Radiances of the Verses

Translation of

Abdul-Latif Bin Abdullah At-Tuwaijiri

First Edition: 2020 CE – 1441 AH

Translated by
Karim Ahmad Safwat

Reviewed & Edited by
Fadhl Hasan

Afaq Al Marefa

Dar Ul Thaqafah

First Edition Published by **Afaq Al Marefa**

www.afaqbooks.com

English Edition Published by **Dar Ul Thaqafah**

www.darulthaqafah.com
www.twitter.com/darulthaqafah

A Subsidiary of **MaktabaIslamia Publications**

www.maktabaislamia.com

Contents

بسم الله الرحمن الرحيم

Dedication

She lives with the Book of Allah through hearing whilst wishing that she knew how to read. She saw me once in an anxious state and said: I do not know how your heart can be constrained whilst you know how to read from the Mus'haf?!

To my dearest mother: Hassa Bint Ibrahim At-Tuwaijiri

May Allah تعالى preserve her.

I dedicate this book to her whilst asking Allah ﷻ that it be correct and accepted.

1441 AH

Introduction to the Radiances (*Al-Mashaariq*)

All praise belongs to Allah in multitudes of praise and goodness, praise that fills the sky covering all regions of the earth, land and sea. And I bear witness that there is no Ilah (deity worthy of worship) other than Allah, alone without a partner. And I bear witness that Muhammad is His slave and Messenger, blessings and peace be upon him, his family and companions altogether.

Thereafter:

Indeed, in the risings of the sun, there are dazzling signs which have adorned the creation with beauty and majesty and beautified it with splendor and magnificence. It is the sun in the centre of the sky shining so that its radiance covers the creation with light and illumination, brilliance and delight.

It is a magnificent manifestation from among the manifestations of divine power and wisdom that appears vividly in the great creation of this Sun:

﴿فَلَا أُقْسِمُ بِرَبِّ الْمَشَارِقِ وَالْمَغَارِبِ إِنَّا لَقَادِرُونَ﴾

"So, I swear by the Lord of all the points of sunrise and sunset in the east and the west that surely We are Able"　　　　　　[TMQ Al-Ma'arij: 40]

The Greatest does not swear oaths except by that which is great!

This is the sun when it rises over the creation with its rays, light and beauty; however, there is another sun and its sunrise is life, its light is splendour, and its rays are warm and endearing.

Indeed, how beautiful is the **"Sun of the Qur'an"** when it rises in the heart of the believer and pervades the breaths of his soul. The heart flies, the spirit soars, and the inner self elevates high. It is the right to rejoice and delight in such a radiance:

﴿قُلْ بِفَضْلِ اللَّهِ وَبِرَحْمَتِهِ فَبِذَٰلِكَ فَلْيَفْرَحُوا هُوَ خَيْرٌ مِّمَّا يَجْمَعُونَ﴾

"Say: "In the Favour of Allah, and His Mercy (i.e. Islam and the Quran); therein let them rejoice". That is better than what they amass (in terms of wealth)"   [TMQ Yunus: 58]

It was reported from Mujaahid, may Allah's mercy be upon him, that he said: [The Fadl (Favour) of Allah is Islam and His Rahmah (Mercy) is the Qur'an][1]. It has been said that: [If the Tafsir of Mujaahid comes to you, then that is sufficient for you!] [2]

How great is the joy of the slave with these two blessings; the blessing of joy with Islam and the blessing of joy with the Qur'an. The axis rests upon the latter as it is this which strengthens the former:

﴿كَذَٰلِكَ لِنُثَبِّتَ بِهِ فُؤَادَكَ وَرَتَّلْنَاهُ تَرْتِيلًا﴾

"Thus (it is sent down in parts), that We may strengthen your heart thereby. And We have revealed it to you gradually, in stages" [TMQ Al-Furqan: 32]

The greatest of creations in terms of firmness and sturdiness are the lofty, towering mountains and yet, despite this strength and solidness, they do not have the strength to contain the brightness of the verses of the Qur'an within their flanks as its sides would be rendered asunder due to the fear of Allah تعالى:

---

[1] Tafsir Al-Maawardi: (2/440).
[2] Tafsir At-Tabari: (1/85).

﴾اَلَوْ أَنزَلْنَا هَٰذَا الْقُرْآنَ عَلَىٰ جَبَلٍ لَّرَأَيْتَهُ خَاشِعًا مُّتَصَدِّعًا مِّنْ خَشْيَةِ اللَّهِ ۚ وَتِلْكَ الْأَمْثَالُ نَضْرِبُهَا لِلنَّاسِ لَعَلَّهُمْ يَتَفَكَّرُونَ﴿

"Had We sent down this Quran on a mountain, you would surely have seen it humbling itself and rending asunder by the fear of Allah. Such are the parables which We put forward to mankind that they may reflect" [TMQ Al-Hashr: 21]

How then would the case be in respect to this small body present within the human being if it were to shine bright?!

When the verses shine bright in the heart of the believer, they radiate upon the limbs manifesting as manners and action. His speech would then be *Noor*, his actions would be *Noor* and his life would be *Noor*.

When the verses shine bright in the heart of the believer, the limbs do not lay ruin, the minds do not behave recklessly, and the *Nafs* (inner self) does not become anxious. That is because they are secure and tranquil in the shade of the exhortations of the Qur'an and the cure of the breasts.

When the verses shine bright in the heart of the believer, he does not devote himself to other than Allah (swt), he does not fear other than Allah (swt) and does not seek other than Allah (swt). That is because his life and his death belong to Allah the Lord of the worlds, who has no partner.

When the verses shine bright in the heart of the believer, the spirit of the slave elevates and rises in the scales of certainty and ascension of *Iman* (belief), and that reassured *Nafs* (self or soul) becomes content and pleasing as a result.

Thereafter, O Blessed one! The domain of these points of radiance is vast, its sun is radiant, and its impact is blessed. However, where are those possessing the pure hearts and minds, those who contemplate and ponder. They are those whom Allah تعالى mentioned in His statement:

﴿كِتَابٌ أَنزَلْنَاهُ إِلَيْكَ مُبَارَكٌ لِّيَدَّبَّرُوا آيَاتِهِ وَلِيَتَذَكَّرَ أُولُو الْأَلْبَابِ﴾

"[This is] a blessed Book which We have revealed to you, [O Muhammad], that they might reflect upon its verses and that those of understanding would be reminded" [TMQ Sad: 29]

The idea of this book "**Mashaariq Al-Aay – Radiances of the Aayaat (Verses)**" came from these introductory points and others beside them for the purpose of inviting the Ummah (Islamic nation) as a whole to live with the *Kitab* (book) of its *Rabb* (Lord), to drink from its spring and ponder upon its meanings. That is because it is this Book which informs them of the features of good and evil, places in their hands the keys to the treasures of happiness, strengthens the *Iman* (belief) in their hearts and provides them with strength, delight, joy and happiness.

This book "**Mashaariq Al-Aay**" (Radiances of the Aayaat (Verses)) is composed of various articles related to the *Nafs* (self), creation and life and has been supported by the statements of the *Awliyaa'* (righteous servants of Allah) and the distinguished masters, coming together to conclude and state: There is no darkness when in the company of the light of the *Wahy* (divine revelation)!

"The points of radiance remind me every day ... That Allah does not leave darkness as it is"!

O Allah, accept it and make it sincerely and purely for your sake, and benefit its writer, compiler, reader and publisher through it. O

Allah, make us all from the people of the Qur'an whom You have favoured. *Allahumma Aameen.*

Abdul-Latif Bin Abdullah At-Tuwaijiri
Riyadh
Rajab, 1441 AH
A44t@hotmail.com

Bringing the Hearts Close Together

"The relation of the womb is severed, the grace of the blessing is ungratefully denied, but we have not seen the like of the hearts being brought together. Allah Says:

$$﴿لَوْ أَنفَقْتَ مَا فِي الْأَرْضِ جَمِيعًا مَّا أَلَّفْتَ بَيْنَ قُلُوبِهِمْ﴾$$

"If you had spent all that is in the earth, you could not have brought their hearts together" [TMQ Al-Anfal: 63]

And that (meaning) is present in the poem:

And I have accompanied the people and then probed them,

And I tested what they reached in terms of relations,

[And found] that the relation by blood does not draw one close definitively,

And that love is the closest of relations"[3]

The interpreter of the Qur'an and scholar of the Ummah Ibn 'Abbas, may Allah be pleased with them both, would not have said that except because bringing hearts together is a matter that baffles thinking and perplexes the mind in relation to what causes it. It is a relationship that surpasses the stretches of history and it is a bond that traverses the borders of lands.

Abu Ash-Sheikh (DoD: 369 AH) related from Al-Awzaa'iy (DoD: 157 AH). He said: Qataadah (DoD: 117 AH) wrote to me:

---

[3] Recorded by Al-Baihaqi in "Shu'ab ul-*Iman*" (11/335). He commented upon it saying: [This is how I found it connected with the statement of Ibn 'Abbas, and I don't know if the statement "And that (meaning) is present in the poem" is from his speech or the statement of someone who has passed by from those narrators].

إن يكن الدهر فرَّق بيننا، فإن أُلْفَة الله الذي ألف بين المسلمين: قريب

"If time has separated between us, then the affection of Allah that He has made between the Muslims is close by" [4]

The wondrous power of Allah تعالى in respect to bringing the hearts together manifests clearly when the brother becomes like the self through it:

﴿لَّوْلَا إِذْ سَمِعْتُمُوهُ ظَنَّ الْمُؤْمِنُونَ وَالْمُؤْمِنَاتُ بِأَنفُسِهِمْ خَيْرًا وَقَالُوا هَٰذَا إِفْكٌ مُّبِينٌ﴾

"Why then, did not the believers, men and women, when you heard it (the slander) think well of their own people and say: "This (charge) is an obvious lie?"*   [TMQ An-Nur: 12] [5]

And giving preference (to others over oneself) becomes a symbol through its taking hold:

﴿وَالَّذِينَ تَبَوَّءُوا الدَّارَ وَالْإِيمَانَ مِن قَبْلِهِمْ يُحِبُّونَ مَنْ هَاجَرَ إِلَيْهِمْ وَلَا يَجِدُونَ فِي صُدُورِهِمْ حَاجَةً مِّمَّا أُوتُوا وَيُؤْثِرُونَ عَلَىٰ أَنفُسِهِمْ وَلَوْ كَانَ بِهِمْ خَصَاصَةٌ﴾

"And those who, before them, had homes (in Al-Madinah) and had adopted the Faith (Iman), love those who emigrate to them, and hold nothing (bad) in their breasts for that which they have been given (i.e. of booty) and they (i.e. Ansar) give them (emigrants) preference over themselves, even though they were suffering privation"* [TMQ Al-Hashr: 9]

When giving preference to others takes hold within a society, that which is distant in it draws near, its remote aspects become close,

---

[4] "Ad-Durr al-Manthur", As-Suyuti (4/101).

[5] Concerning the statement in the Ayah (An-Nur: 12): It means why did they (The male and female believers) not think well of their brothers. Refer to the Tafsir of At-Tabari: (17/211)

its people become connected to one another, and peace predominates. Bringing the hearts together is, therefore, the key to their purification and the precursor to their purity. This is what the society of Al-Madinah was like during the time of the Messenger of Allah ﷺ and as such, it represents the clear proof and manifest evidence.

Drawing the hearts together leads to the flourishing of the *Akhlaq* (morals), the expansion of the values and the increase of *Iman*:

لاَ يُؤْمِنُ أَحَدُكُمْ حَتَّى يُحِبَّ لأَخِيهِ مَا يُحِبُّ لِنَفْسِهِ

None of you believes until he loves for his brother what he loves for himself [6].

How can it be possible for the love of goodness to arise if the hearts have not been brought together?! Or how is it possible for honour, giving and charity to become widespread if the selves are not cleaned and purified?!

Bringing together the hearts reflects: A mixing amongst the souls and an embrace between the hearts. There is no place in it for appearances or formalities. The final decisive word regarding it is: **"Love for your brother like that which you love for yourself"**.

It is a miraculous melting pot in which historical envy, tribal acts of vengeance, greedy personal ambitions and racist banners are dissolved and melt away.

Bringing together the hearts: Is a blessing that Allah bestowed upon the honourable companions.

---

[6] Recorded by Al-Bukhari in the *Kitab* of Al-*Iman*, under the heading: "It is from *Iman* to love for his brother what he loves for himself", Hadith: 13. Muslim recorded it in the *Kitab* of Al-*Iman*, under the heading: "The evidence that loving for your brother is from the attributes of *Iman*", Hadith: 45.

Allah تعالى said when bestowing it upon them:

﴿وَاذْكُرُوا نِعْمَتَ اللَّهِ عَلَيْكُمْ إِذْ كُنتُمْ أَعْدَاءً فَأَلَّفَ بَيْنَ قُلُوبِكُمْ فَأَصْبَحْتُم بِنِعْمَتِهِ إِخْوَانًا﴾

"And remember the favour of Allah upon you - when you were enemies and He brought your hearts together and you became, by His blessing, brothers"   [Aali 'Imran: 103]

The mind should allow its thinking to flow to allow it to ponder upon this *Aayah* (verse), and to contemplate the connection between bringing the hearts together and the greatest blessing, which is the *Iman* (belief) in Allah تعالى. That is because the preceding verses mention Allah's divine bestowal of the blessing of *Iman*:

﴿يَا أَيُّهَا الَّذِينَ آمَنُوا اتَّقُوا اللَّهَ حَقَّ تُقَاتِهِ وَلَا تَمُوتُنَّ إِلَّا وَأَنتُم مُّسْلِمُونَ﴾

"O you who have believed, fear Allah as He should be feared and do not die except as Muslims [in submission to Him]"   [TMQ Aali 'Imran: 102]

That is because these two represent the greatest pillars in respect to the building of the Islamic society. Indeed, they exemplified the greatest pillar for establishing the first state of Islam, which was a source of revitalisation for the world and a radiant sun for humanity.

That formation of brotherhood which the Messenger ﷺ initiated his actions with in the new land of emigration represents the source of every brotherhood in Islam, in all times and places, just as Ibn 'Atiyah (DoD: 542 AH) said:

"And every bringing together in Islam is a consequence of that bringing together that took place at the inception of Islam"[7]

Drawing hearts close together is the most significant task of those who love good for the people. It is for that reason that it was among the earliest of the Prophetic actions related to the establishment and formation of the state. It is from the actions of the pioneers and leaders. Discussing it is not an indulgence but rather an essential matter. The *Maslahah* (interest and well-being) of the Ummah dictates it, the *Maslahah* (interest) of the individual makes it necessary, and sincerity to everyone obliges it.

The key to bringing hearts together is *"Ad-Deen Al-Haqq"* (The *Deen* of truth), and its most singular secret is the presence of the "Good relationship with Allah تعلى". When our relationship with Allah is good, Allah makes our relationship with the people good. Any other basis for bringing hearts together is a mirage that the thirsty believes to be water that dissipates at the nearest problem, disappears at the first trial and test, and then, in the end, it becomes a source of sorrow and regret:

﴿وَقَالَ إِنَّمَا اتَّخَذْتُم مِّن دُونِ اللَّهِ أَوْثَانًا مَّوَدَّةَ بَيْنِكُمْ فِي الْحَيَاةِ الدُّنْيَا ۖ ثُمَّ يَوْمَ الْقِيَامَةِ يَكْفُرُ بَعْضُكُم بِبَعْضٍ وَيَلْعَنُ بَعْضُكُم بَعْضًا وَمَأْوَاكُمُ النَّارُ وَمَا لَكُم مِّن نَّاصِرِينَ﴾

"And [Ibrahim] said, "You have only taken, instead of Allah, idols as [a bond of] affection among you in the worldly life. Then on the Day of Resurrection you will deny one another and curse one another, and your abode will be the Fire, and you shall have no helper" [TMQ Al-Ankabut: 25]

---

[7] Tafsir Ibn 'Atiyah (2/548-549).

At-Tabari (DoD: 310 AH), in his Tafsir, attributed the following to 'Abdah bin Abi Lubabah (DoD: 127 AH) (رحمه الله) from Mujahid (DoD: 102 AH), whom he had met and received knowledge directly from, that he said: [If two people who love each other for the sake of Allah (in Islam) exist, where one of them takes the hand of his friend (in support) and smiles at him, their sins will drop from them just like the leaves of the tree fall. 'Abdah said to him: Indeed, this is an easy matter (to accomplish). He replied: Do not say that because Allah says:

$$﴿لَوْ أَنفَقْتَ مَا فِي الْأَرْضِ جَمِيعًا مَّا أَلَّفْتَ بَيْنَ قُلُوبِهِمْ﴾$$

"If you had spent all that is in the earth, you could not have brought their hearts together"　　　　　　　　　　　　　　　　　　[TMQ Al-Anfal: 63]

'Abdah said: It was at that instant that I knew that he had a greater understanding than me. [8]

This understanding that he (رحمه الله) possessed was only due to his knowledge of the situation of the *Jahiliyah* (pre-Islamic period) and what existed amongst the people in terms of grudges and throwing themselves into acts of vengeance, making it virtually impossible for even two hearts to be brought together. It was for this reason that the Arabs did not establish states possessing sovereignty before the advent of Islam [9].

He understood the true realities of what exists within the people and the essences of the hearts. That is genuinely worthy of being called understanding. It is an understanding that elevates the souls towards bringing them together and towards love, guidance, and righteousness. It is the understanding that brings together and

---

[8] Tafsir Tabari (11/258)
[9] Refer to: Tafsir Az-Zamakhshari: (2/233-234) and Tafsir Al-Baidawi: (3/65).

does not divide, pardons and does not set people against each other. It strives its utmost to spread forbearance, sincerity among one another and to establish close relations among the people and the individuals of the society.

Drawing hearts close together is from among the aims of the Islamic legislation, which the one who contemplates can perceive within the statement of the Imam of prayer when he says: **"Align with one another and do not differ so that your hearts are not made to differ"**. This aligning and bringing of the bodies close together in the prayers in our Masajid reflects a sign indicating to the requirement to bring the hearts together within the life which we live as a whole. It represents a legislative exhortation to avoid discord and exiting from the Millah (i.e. the *Deen* of Islam), may we seek refuge in Allah from desires and rebellious disobedience.

The Qur'an and the *Tarbiyyah* (Nurturing) upon Sound Behaviour and Manners

As-Sakhawiy (DoD: 902 AH) related from Al-Muzani (the student of Ash-Shafi'iy) that he said: [Ash-Shafi'iy (DoD: 204 AH) was teaching me one day, and I said: "So and so person is a liar". He said to me: "O Abu Ibrahim, characterize your words with the best of them. Do not say: So and so person is a liar. But rather say: His speech does not carry any weight"] [10].

How great is this education which is wrapped in manners (*Al-Adab*) and adorned with morals (*Al-Akhlaq*)! This is how the teachers should be, and Ash-Shafi'iy is sufficient for you as a teacher and educator.

The statement "Characterize your words with the best of them" reflects educational guidance which directs thought towards the usages or customs (*'Aadaat*) of the Qur'an, which the *Salaf* (predecessors), may Allah have mercy upon them, deduced from the shades of its verses. This is like what is found in the narration which Imam At-Tabari (DoD: 310 AH) attributed to Mujahid (DoD: 102 AH), may Allah have mercy upon him, in relation to Allah's statement:

$$﴿يَضْرِبُونَ وُجُوهَهُمْ وَأَدْبَارَهُمْ﴾$$

"They strike their faces and their backs"　　　　　　　　[Al-Anfal: 50]

He said: "And their backsides! However, Allah is Karim and uses indirect expressions" [11].

---

[10] Fat'h ul-Mugheeth, As-Sakhawiy: (2/128).
[11] Tafsir At-Tabari: (11/230).

Thoroughly studying and examining the Qur'an Al-Karim is the methodological approach of the *Salaf* (predecessors) in relation to *At-Taddabur* (Thinking deeply and contemplating upon the verses). It is possible that some of those who came later named this *"'Aadaat ul-Qur'aan"* (The usages or customs of the Qur'an). Az-Zarkashiy (DoD: 794 AH) said:

من عادة القرآن العظيم الكناية عن الجماع باللمس والملامسة والرفث والدخول

والنكاح ونحوهن...

"It is from the customary usage ('Aadah) of the Qur'an Al-Karim to use the indirect expression (Al-*Kinayah*) for the act of sexual relations by using (the wordings) touch (Lams), mutual touching (Mulaamasah), Ar-Rafath (a metaphor for a man approaching his wife used to avoid any crudeness), entering (Ad-Dukhool), An-Nikaah (taken from mixing like the rain water mixing in the soil) and other such terms ..." [12].

Ash-Shaatibiy (DoD: 790) said:

أتى فيه [القرآن] الكناية في الأمور التي يُستحيى من التصريح بها... فاستقر ذلك

أدبًا لنا استنبطناه من هذه المواضع، وإنما دلالتها على هذه المعاني بحكم التبع لا

بالأصل

"The *Kinayah* (metaphor or indirect expression) came in it (Al-Qur'an) in matters which one is shy or ashamed to be explicit in expression concerning them ... That then settled to be a manner of conduct (*Adab*) for us. We deduced it from these contextual places.

---

[12] Al-Burhan Fee 'Uloom ul-Qur'an, Az-Zarkashi: (2/303-304).

They are indicative of these meanings only in accordance with the rule of following (*At-Taba'a*) and not that of the origin (Al-Asl)" [13].

This thorough examination does not take place except by expending effort in respect to understanding the Qur'an and living in its shade. In this guidance, he (Ash-Shafi'iy, may Allah's mercy be upon him) wants to place the Ummah, via the educational direction of the Qur'an, upon the use of wholesome speech and for the best of it to be selected. That is especially the case when speaking about that which one is shy or ashamed to speak about:

فكل كلمات القرآن بلا استثناء هي أعلى الألفاظ وأرفع الأساليب، فلا نجد في القرآن كلمة لا تليق، ولا كلمة تخدش الحياء، ولا نرى عبارة لا تتسم بالأدب

"All of the words of the Qur'an, without exception, represent the highest worded expressions and the most elevated of styles. We do not find in the Qur'an any word which is not fitting, nor any word that violates or offends the sense of shame, just as we do not find any expression that is not harmonious with the *Adab* (best manners)" [14].

It is fitting for the believer for the customary usages of the Qur'an to be a school for him, the basis for moral conduct and the model for life, emulating in this our Prophet Muhammad ﷺ whose manners and conduct were the (manifestation of the) Qur'an, as was mentioned in the description of A'aishah, may Allah be pleased with her.

---

[13] Al-Muwaafaqaat, Ash-Shaatibiy: (2/165).

[14] 'Aadaat Al-Qur'an Al-Usloobiyah, Hamoud Ath-Thanayaan: (1/168)

This noble Quranic usage elevates the tongues of the believers and purifies their expressions. It reflects the embodiment of the Muslim personality, the clear proof and evidence of civilisation, the mark of the mind and the magnificence of manners and moral conduct.

Here we find the Quranic precedence in paying heed to what is called sound and refined conduct and manners, before it was known to the west and philosophers. If refined conduct and manners in the west were confined in their societies to the upper classes, the educational guidance of the Qur'an upon such conduct and manners was for the entire Ummah, without any consideration to the class or any other differentiation. From this, we can understand the care of Ash-Shafi'iy (DoD: 204 AH), may Allah's mercy be upon him, to educate his student to employ grace in words and beauty in the manner of speaking.

It is well known that Imam Al-Bukhari (DoD: 256 AH), may Allah's mercy be upon him, was an Imam (scholar) in *Al-Jarh and At-Ta'deel* (critiquing and scrutinising the authenticity of the Hadith and their narrators) and that his expressions flowed with manners, as Ibn Hajar (DoD: 852 AH) testified to, when he said: [That Al-Bukhari in his speech concerning the narrators gave additional care (or caution) and utilised a profound manner of examination, for the one who ponders upon his speech, in his critique of the narrators (*Al-Jarh and At-Ta'deel*). How often he would say: "They were silent concerning him", or "He is examined" (i.e. there are issues concerning him that need to be looked into), or "They left him" (i.e. did not narrate from him) and similar such expressions. And how little he would say: "He is a liar" or "Fabricator". He would only say: "Such and such a person said he was a liar" or "Such and such accused him (i.e. of lying)"] [15].

And you, if you were to contemplate their circumstances, you would have found that the graceful word reflected a bridge based upon manners and an elevated disposition which extended to the gatherings of the *'Ulamaa* (scholars) and the *Salaf* (predecessors) and was from the inheritance of the Prophethood. Consequently, wherever knowledge was present, manners were present alongside them, just as high-minded and intelligent speech were in attendance.

It has been told that from the intelligence of the Khalifah Al-Ma'mun (DoD: 218 AH) during his childhood, was his polite and good speech. His father Harun Ar-Rasheed (DoD: 193 AH) used to favour him and gave him priority over his brother Al-Amin, leading his wife Zubaidah (DoD: 216 AH) to reproach him for that. He then said to her in the way of an excuse: "I will make evident to you from their circumstances that which excuses me in respect to him". He then summoned Al-Amin, and he had small sticks (*Miswak*) with him and asked him: "What is this O Muhammad?" He replied: "Small sticks (Miswak)". He then said: "Leave". He then summoned Al-Ma'mun and asked him: "What is this of Abdullah?" He replied: "It is in opposition to your good qualities, O Leader of the Believers". It was also related that he said to him: "The bad qualities of your enemies, O Leader of the Believers". Zubaidah heard all of that and accepted his excuse [16].

The one who contemplates the Islamic society, in its generality, finds that it infuses refined manners and polite speech. The public

---

[15] Fat'h ul-Baari': (1/480).
[16] Refer to: "Qiladah An-Nahr Fee Wafayat A'ayaan Ad-Dahr", Al-Hadramiy (2/469).

manners then become elevated and the polite word (speech) becomes an important pillar of its civilisation. This was expressed best by the poet Al-Mutanabbi (DoD: 354 AH) when he said:

You have no horse and no wealth to gift

So, let the speech assist if the means do not assist!

An-Nawawi (DoD: 676 AH), in a general account and fine comment introducing his writing, said: [And from that which has been forbidden is: Obscenity and foulness of the tongue ... Kinayaat (indirect expressions) should be used in relation to that and they should be expressed by way of a beautiful (or nice) expression, from which the meaning or purpose is understood. It was with this style that the Qur'an Al-'Azeez and the Noble Sahih (authentic) Sunnah came ... The *'Ulamaa* (scholars) said: In this and what resembles it in terms of expressions, which one is shamed to mention by its explicit name, indirect expressions (Kinayaat) which provide the understanding should be used ... Similarly, the mention of blemishes or abnormalities like leprosy, halitosis and body odour, should be expressed with nice expressions from which the meaning is understood. And what is similar to what we have mentioned in terms of examples joins them (i.e. they follow the same principle).

Know that all of this applies if there is no need to use its explicit name. If the need requires that for the purpose of explanation and teaching and it is feared that the one being spoken to will not understand the metaphor or that he will understand other than its intended meaning, then in such circumstances, the explicit name is used to make sure that the correct understanding is attained.

The Ahadeeth which have come with explicit statements are understood upon this basis][17].

Therefore, O intelligent one: Always pay special attention to the pureness of your speech and the wholesomeness of your expressions. Dress them with beauty and kindness. Through that, you will elevate, and you will be drinking from the Qur'an. Remember, that in Al-Jannah (paradise): **"There are chambers the inside of which can be seen from the outside and the outside can be seen from the inside"** and that is the reward for the one who **"Speaks (good) kind words,** feeds people and prays to Allah at night when people are asleep" [18].

---

[17] Al-Adhkaar, An-Nawawi (p375-376).

[18] Recorded by At-Tirmidhi from the Hadith of 'Ali bin Abi Talib, may Allah be pleased with him, under the chapter heading of 'Righteous Conduct and Maintaining the Ties', the sub-chapter of 'What came in relation to Qawl Al-Ma'roof (the good speech)', Hadith number (1984). It was also recorded by Imam Ahmad in his Musnad, in the Musnad (attributed heading) of Al-Khulafa' Ar-Rashideen, the Musnad of 'Ali bin Abi Talib, Hadith number (1338). Al-Albani classified it as Sahih (authentic) in Mishkaat Al-Masabeeh (1/388).

A Hardship Will Never Overcome Two Eases

Adversities rage over nations just as they rage over individuals. The life of nations is an enlarged copy of the life of individuals, however the calamities of nations are greater and more severe. For that reason, thinking becomes confused in the midst of its dilemmas and consequently requires guidance, light, direction and instruction.

At-Tabari (DoD: 310 AH) related in his Tafsir concerning Abu 'Ubaidah bin Al-Jarrah in relation to the statement of Allah تعالى:

﴿يَا أَيُّهَا الَّذِينَ آمَنُوا اصْبِرُوا وَصَابِرُوا وَرَابِطُوا وَاتَّقُوا اللَّهَ لَعَلَّكُمْ تُفْلِحُونَ﴾

"O you who have believed, be patient, persevere, remain stationed (guarding the frontiers) and fear Allah that you may be successful"

[TMQ Aali 'Imran: 200]

That he (Abu 'Ubaidah) wrote to 'Umar ibn Al-Khattab and mentioned to him the large army of Romans and what he feared from them. 'Umar then wrote back to him: "Thereafter, however much a believing slave descends into a situation of severity (and hardship), Allah makes for him after that a way out or relief, and verily a hardship will never overcome two eases. Indeed, Allah, the most glorified, the highest, says in His Book:

﴿يَا أَيُّهَا الَّذِينَ آمَنُوا اصْبِرُوا وَصَابِرُوا وَرَابِطُوا وَاتَّقُوا اللَّهَ لَعَلَّكُمْ تُفْلِحُونَ﴾

"O you who have believed, be patient, persevere, remain stationed (guarding the frontiers) and fear Allah that you may be successful"

We decipher in this concise response of 'Umar, how he lived with the Qur'an, how 'Umar lived with the radiances of the verses and their guidance. As such, we do not find anxiety at the time of hardship, surrender to the creation (i.e. man), nor the seeking of a truce.

This is the effect of the Qur'an upon its companion. Therefore, the fruit of living with the Qur'an at the time of ease and comfort provides its companion with strength, perseverance, peace and tranquillity during the time of hardship, and the Qur'an never lets down its companion!

In the response of 'Umar, may Allah be pleased with him, we find how the believer suffices himself alone with the Qur'an Al-Karim, which reflects one of the meanings of the statement of the Messenger ﷺ in the Hadeeth related by Abu Hurairah, may Allah be pleased with him:

$$\text{لَيْسَ مِنَّا مَنْ لَمْ يَتَغَنَّ بِالْقُرْآنِ}$$

The one who does not suffice himself with the Qur'an is not one of us [20].

This means to be sufficed and satisfied with the Qur'an from anything other than it, as was mentioned in the Tafsir of Imam Sufyan bin 'Uyainah (DoD: 198 AH) [21]. And what sufficing with the

---

[19] Tafsir At-Tabari (6/334).

[20] Al-Bukhari, *Kitab* At-Tawhid, Chapter: The speech of Allah تعالى: (وَأَسِرُّوا قَوْلَكُمْ
أُو اجْهَرُوا بِهِ) [And whether you keep your talk secret or disclose it: Al-Mulk: 13], Hadith number: (7527)

[21] Refer to: "Fat'h ul-Baari", Ibn Hajar (9/68)

Qur'an is better than that which is done in decisions related to the Ummah and its policies?! The Qur'an which produced the generation of the Sahabah (companions) will produce generations of the Ummah if it suffices itself with the Qur'an like the generation of the Sahabah did.

In order to be sufficed with the Qur'an, it must be thought deeply upon and acted upon. There are, therefore, two fundamental pillars:

The first: Understanding, and that is apparent in the tradition through his ('Umar's, may Allah be pleased with him) interpretation of Ar-Ribaat in connection to *Al-Muraabatah* (being stationed in defense of the frontiers) in the way of Allah, just as the majority of the *Mufassireen* (Scholars of Tafsir) have interpreted it. [22]

The second: Action, and in this tradition (narration) it is found in his instruction to Abu Ubaidah and the Muslim army under his command to act upon it.

Included among the amazing features of this tradition and its lessons is: The knowledge related to the application of the verses upon the reality of the Muslims to make it feasible for them to act in accordance with it. Just as this reflects the pillar of deep thought (*At-Tadabbur*), it also represents the ultimate aim. Al-Hasan Al-Basriy (DoD: 110 AH), may Allah have mercy upon him, said:

وما تدبرُ آياتِه إلا اتباعُه بعلمِه، والله ما هو بحفظ حروفه وإضاعة حدوده...

"The deep thinking and pondering (*Tadabbur*) upon its verses is not manifested except by following it (in terms of action) based

---

upon the understanding of it. By Allah, it is not manifested by memorizing its letters and neglecting its limits ..." [23].

Applying the verses to the reality requires *Fiqh* (understanding). It is, therefore a duty upon the one seeking to contemplate upon the Qur'an to seek this tool and to acquire the necessary areas of knowledge that he needs in order to think deeply upon the Qur'an Al-Karim.

مهما نزَل بعبدٍ مؤمنٍ من منزلةِ شدة، يجعَلُ اللهُ بعدها فرجًا

"However much a believing slave descends into a situation of severity (and hardship), Allah makes for him after that a way out or relief".

This statement (of 'Umar's) demonstrates the skill of introducing a matter (or concept) as it includes a preparation for the souls and training them upon patience. Then the reminder concerning the relief (after the hardship) is to lighten the bitterness of the patience and the weight of the obligations.

"And verily a hardship will never overcome two eases".

That is because Allah تعالى said:

﴿فَإِنَّ مَعَ الْعُسْرِ يُسْرًا * إِنَّ مَعَ الْعُسْرِ يُسْرًا﴾

"So verily, with the hardship, there is relief, (5) Verily, with the hardship, there is relief" (i.e. there is one hardship with two reliefs, so one hardship cannot overcome two reliefs) [TMQ Ash-Sharh: 5-6]

This reflects the disposition of 'Umar, may Allah be pleased with him, manifested in this share that he has been given of guidance.

---

[23] Recorded by Abdur Razzaq in his Musannaf, the book of Fadaa'il (Virtues of) Al-Qur'an, chapter: Ta'aahud Al-Qur'an (3/363).

It reflects an acquisition gained from the light of the verses and it also includes certainty in the promise of Allah, which cannot be concealed from the one who observes and experienced hardships and suffered distresses. He was aware that this certainty with the promise of Allah does not occur with everyone. That is because the certainty in Allah at the time of hardship is the relief in itself, whilst the door to attain the certainty, as stated by Ibn Taymiyah (DoD: 728 AH), is the *Tadabbur* (the deep thought and contemplation) upon the Qur'an Al-Karim [24].

Indeed, from among the greatest encouragements to persevere upon the *Haqq* (truth) is: Being reminded by the Qur'an Al-'Azheem as Allah تعالى said:

﴿فَذَكِّرْ بِالْقُرْآنِ مَن يَخَافُ وَعِيدِ﴾

"So, remind by the Qur'an whoever fears My threat"　　　[TMQ Qaaf: 45]

Therefore, how much we are in need of this Quranic reminder among ourselves just as was the way of those great distinguished personalities (i.e. the Sahabah), may Allah be pleased with them all.

---

[24] Majmoo' Al-Fataawaa. Sheikh ul-Islam Ibn Taymiyah (3/330).

The Entirety of the *Sharee'ah* is Beneficial and for the Well-Being

The *Sharee'ah* of Islam represents the interests from the *Rabb* (lord) to His servants, just as was stated by Ash-Sheikh Al-'Izz bin Abdus Salaam (DoD: 660 AH)[25] , may Allah's mercy be upon him. It is upon this principle that all branches of the *Sharee'ah* in all areas of *Fiqh* are dependent: *'Ibaadaat* (worships), *Mu'aamalaat* (societal transactions), *Hudood* (prescribed punishments) and *Jinaayaat* (crimes).

This objective reading of the *Ahkam Ash-Shar'iyah* is derived from the Shar'iyah texts and the narrated traditions of the *Salaf* (predecessors) disseminated across the recorded Islamic writings. Imam At-Tabari (DoD: 310 AH), in his Tafsir, attributed to Qataadah (DoD: 117 AH), may Allah's mercy be upon him, that he said in connection to the *Qawl* of Allah تعالى:

﴿وَالسَّارِقُ وَالسَّارِقَةُ فَاقْطَعُوا أَيْدِيَهُمَا جَزَاءً بِمَا كَسَبَا نَكَالًا مِّنَ اللَّهِ ۗ وَاللَّهُ عَزِيزٌ حَكِيمٌ﴾

"And the male thief and the female thief, amputate their hands in recompense for what they committed as a deterrent [punishment] from Allah. And Allah is Exalted in Might and Wise"   [TMQ Al-Ma'idah: 38]

He said:

لا تَرْثُوا لهم أَن تُقِيمُوا فيهم الحدود، فإنه والله ما أمرَ اللهُ بأمرٍ قطُّ إلا وهو صلاح، ولا نَهى عن أمرٍ قطُّ إلا وهو فساد

Do not bemoan that the *Hudood* (prescribed punishments) be implemented amongst them, for verily and by Allah, Allah did not command any matter at all except that it is beneficial (and for the well-being) and He did not forbid any matter at all except that it was corruption (or contained harm) [26].

The divine *Hudood* (prescribed punishments) like that related to theft, as referred to above, or the punishment for the fornicator or that of stoning amongst other similar rulings have become a focal point for atheists and orientalists to stir doubts within people. Sometimes that is by claiming that these punishments are harsh, sometimes they claim that they are at odds with personal freedoms and on other occasions that they clash with the happenings of modern contemporary life and its newly occurring realities.

Such specious arguments (or raised doubts) in past ages only use to reach limited audiences, however, today with the major technological breakthrough that has taken place such arguments reach people in their homes and when they are alone! That is because people can broadcast these specious arguments across the open airwaves and as such the new generations have come to be bombarded by waves of these raised doubts and specious arguments (*Shubuhaat*) in a frightening chaotic spectacle.

Here comes the role of intellectual fortification and its importance, just Al-Khalil (Ibrahim (عليه السلام)) said:

$$ ﴿وَلَٰكِن لِّيَطْمَئِنَّ قَلْبِي﴾ $$

---

[26] Tafsir At-Tabari (8/410).

"(Yes), but so that my heart is further reassured" [TMQ Al-Baqarah: 260]

From among the most important ways of intellectual fortification is:

زيادة اليقين لدى أفراد الأمة.

Increasing the *Yaqeen* (certainty) among the individuals of the Ummah.

Al-Imam Ibn Taymiyah (DoD: 728 AH) explained the ways of attaining *Yaqeen* when he said: [(It occurs through three matters: Firstly: Deep thought and contemplation upon the Qur'an. Secondly: Thinking deeply and contemplating the signs which Allah has created in the people (Anfus) and the horizons which make evident that He is *Haqq* (truth). Thirdly: To act in accordance with knowledge ('Ilm)] [27].

A demonstration of *At-Tadabbur* (deep thought) upon the Qur'an through which certainty (*Yaqeen*) is attained among the Ummah is found in the previously mentioned tradition of Qataadah (DoD: 117 AH). This is where he clearly determined that there is well-being and benefit for the Ummah and the individuals within the *Hudood* (prescribed punishments). The settling of this legislative principle in the heart of the Muslim leads him to have *Yaqeen* in his *Deen*, firmness upon it, *Iman* (certain belief) in his *Shar'a* and pride in his identity.

These *Hudood* (prescribed punishments) are for the well-being of the servants and a mercy for them. That is because Allah sent Muhammad ﷺ only as a mercy for mankind and He, glorified be

---

[27] Majmoo' Al-Fataawaa, Sheikh ul-Islam Ibn Taymiyah (3/330-331).

He, is more merciful with His servants than the mother is with her child. However, the due mercy may not be attained unless it is accompanied by some form of suffering or hardship that reaches some of the people. That is like what came mentioned in the reported tradition: [When they say to the sick person: "O Allah have mercy upon him". Allah says:

إذا قالوا للمريض اللهم ارحمه، يقول الله: كيف أَرْحمُهُ من شيء به أرحمُهُ!

"How do I bestow mercy upon him from a matter that I am already bestowing my mercy upon him with!" [28]. In the same way, the *Hudood* (prescribed punishments) are a mercy upon the perpetrator and a protection for the Ummah and the well-being of the society.

The angle of well-being within these prescribed punishments for the "Perpetrator of the major sins (*Kabaa'ir*)" is that they act as a *Kaffaarah* (expiation) and purification for him. That is in accordance with what came stated in the Hadith of 'Ubaadah bin As-Saamit, may Allah be pleased with him, as recorded by Muslim. He said: We were gathered with the Messenger of Allah ﷺ and he said:

تُبَايِعُونِي عَلَى أَنْ لاَ تُشْرِكُوا بِاللَّهِ شَيْئًا وَلاَ تَزْنُوا وَلاَ تَسْرِقُوا وَلاَ تَقْتُلُوا النَّفْسَ الَّتِي حَرَّمَ اللَّهُ إِلاَّ بِالْحَقِّ فَمَنْ وَفَى مِنْكُمْ فَأَجْرُهُ عَلَى اللَّهِ وَمَنْ أَصَابَ شَيْئًا مِنْ ذَلِكَ فَعُوقِبَ بِهِ فَهُوَ كَفَّارَةٌ لَهُ وَمَنْ أَصَابَ شَيْئًا مِنْ ذَلِكَ فَسَتَرَهُ اللَّهُ عَلَيْهِ فَأَمْرُهُ إِلَى اللَّهِ إِنْ شَاءَ عَفَا عَنْهُ وَإِنْ شَاءَ عَذَّبَهُ

---

[28] Al Istiqama, Ibn Taymiyyah (1/440)

"Swear allegiance to me that you will not associate anything with Allah, that you will not commit *Zina* (fornication or adultery), that you will not steal, that you will not take any life which Allah has forbidden you to take unless it is with (legal) justification; and whoever among you fulfils it, his reward is with Allah and he who commits any such thing and is punished for it, then that will be an expiation (*Kaffaarah*) for him. And if anyone commits anything and Allah conceals (his faults), then his matter rests with Allah. He may forgive him if He wishes, and He may punish him if He wishes" [29].

An-Nawawi (DoD: 676 AH), may Allah's mercy be upon him, said:

من ارتكب ذنبًا يوجب الحد؛ فحُدَّ سقط عنه الإثم

"Whoever perpetrated a crime that obliges the imposition of the Hadd (prescribed punishment), then the Hadd removes the sin from him".

Al-Qaadi 'Iyaad (DoD: 544 AH) said:

قال القاضي عياض [ت: 544]: قال أكثر العلماء: الحدود كفارة

"Most of the *'Ulamaa* (scholars) have said: Al-*Hudood* (prescribed punishments) are a *Kaffaarah* (expiation for the sins)"] [30].

The punishment of the *Dunyaa* (life of this world) is insignificant in comparison to the punishment of the hereafter and the rational person prioritises the lesser of the two harms over the greater of them.

---

[29] Recorded by Muslim in the Book of Al-*Hudood*, in the chapter heading "The *Hudood* are a Kaffaarah (expiation) for those they are applied upon", Hadith number: 1709.

[30] Sharh An-Nawawi of (Sahih) Muslim, (11/224).

As for the society and the Ummah, then the prescribed punishments represent the safety valve for them, just as the Fuqahaa' (jurists), may Allah have mercy upon them, said:

وحدود الشرع موانع قبل الوقوع، وزواجر بعده

[The *Hudood* of the *Shar'a* are preventers before their occurrence and deterrents after it] [31].

Knowledge of them deters the crime due to the fear of physical suffering whilst their implementation acts as a preventative deterrent for its reoccurrence. That is as the *Hikmah* (wisdom) of its legislation as stated by Az-Zai'la'iy Al-Hanafiy (DoD: 743 AH) is:

الانزجار عما يتضرر به العباد، وصيانة دار الإسلام عن الفساد؛ ولهذا كان حقًّا

لله تعالى؛ لأنه شرع لمصلحة تعود إلى كافة الناس

"To deter that which brings harm to the servants and to protect the land of Islam from corruption. For this reason, it is a right belonging to Allah تعالى as it was legislated for the benefit (*Maslahah*) that returns to all of the people" [32].

And Allah تعالى made from the injunctions of the *Hudood* that which deters the ignorant person due to wariness associated with suffering the pain of the punishment and due to fear of the exemplary punishment of the disgraceful act. This is so that what He prohibited in terms of His prohibitions continue to be refrained from and what He has commanded in terms of His obligations continue to be followed. The *Maslahah* (interest and benefit) would

---

[31] Al-Binaayah Sharh Al-Hidaayah, Al-'Ainiy. (6/256).

[32] Tabyeen Al-Haqaa'iq, (3/163).

therefore be more widespread and the legal responsibility more complete. Allah تعالى said:

$$﴿وَمَا أَرْسَلْنَاكَ إِلَّا رَحْمَةً لِّلْعَالَمِينَ﴾$$

"And we have not sent you except as a mercy for the worlds (mankind)"

[TMQ Al-Anbiya: 107]

This means to save them from ignorance, to steer them away from misguidance, to deter them from the acts of disobedience and to encourage them upon obedience [33].

Qatadah (DoD: 117) was truthful in the aforementioned reported tradition when he said:

$$فإنه والله ما أمرَ اللهُ بأمرٍ قطُّ إلا وهو صلاح، ولا نهى عن أمرٍ قطُّ إلا وهو فساد$$

Verily and by Allah, Allah did not command any matter at all except that it is beneficial (and for the well-being) and He did not forbid a matter at all except that it was corruption (or contained harm.

---

[33] Al-Ahkam As-Sultaaniyah, Al-Maawardiy (p 325).

The Soundness of the Role Models and Examples

From among the pillars of reform is to begin from the peak of the pyramid which means to start with the role models. That is because the soundness and uprightness of the people is found in their soundness and uprightness. If they become corrupted, then the people follow them in that regard. Yahya bin Abi Kathir (DoD: 129 AH), may Allah's mercy be upon him, said: "The *'Ulamaa* (Scholars) like salt, it is for the good of everything, but if the salt becomes corrupted nothing can rectify it" [34]. Al-Imam Sufyan Ath-Thawri (DoD: 161 AH), may Allah's mercy be upon him, when asked: "What thing or matter is worst?", he answered:

اللهم غَفْرًا! العلماء إذا فسدوا

"O Allah, I seek your forgiveness! The *'Ulamaa* if they become corrupted" [35].

The danger of the corruption of the scholars is made evident in what came mentioned in relation to the warning about the slips of the scholar. Ibn 'Abbaas, may Allah be pleased with them both, said: "Woe to those who follow the slips (mistakes) of the scholar". It was asked: "How does that occur?". He said: "A scholar says something that fits a person's opinion and then that person finds someone who is more knowledge with the (knowledge of the) Messenger of Allah ﷺ than him but he leaves his opinion and continues following (the original opinion)" [36].

---

[34] Hulyah Al-Awliyah, Abu Nu'aim (3/67).

[35] Hulyah Al-Awliyah, Abu Nu'aim (7/5).

[36] Jaami' Bayaan Al-'Ilm Wa Fadlihi, Ibn Abdul Barr, (2/984).

If this is the situation in respect to the slip of the scholar, then the situation is graver in respect to the scholars abandoning their roles in relation to commanding the *Ma'roof* (good) and forbidding the *Munkar* (evil), as was mentioned in the reported tradition recorded by Al-Imam At-Tabari (DoD: 310 AH) and attributed to Ad-Dahhaak (DoD: 102), may Allah's mercy be upon him, concerning His statement تعالى:

﴿لَوْلَا يَنْهَاهُمُ الرَّبَّانِيُّونَ وَالْأَحْبَارُ عَن قَوْلِهِمُ الْإِثْمَ وَأَكْلِهِمُ السُّحْتَ ۚ لَبِئْسَ مَا كَانُوا يَصْنَعُونَ﴾

"Why do the rabbis and religious scholars not forbid them from saying what is sinful and devouring what is unlawful? How wretched is what they have been practicing" [TMQ Al-Ma'idah: 63]

He (Ad-Dahhaak) said:

ما في القرآن آيةٌ أخوف عندي منها، أنَّا لا نَنْهَى!

There is no verse in the Qur'an that is more frightening to me than it, that we refrain from forbidding! [37].

The secret behind Ad-Dahhaak's fear from the verse, as is apparent, and Allah knows best, was his understanding of the rebuke contained within it. Al-Qurtubi (DoD: 102 AH) said:

فالآية توبيخ للعلماء في ترك الأمر بالمعروف والنهي عن المنكر

---

[37] Tafsir Al-Qurtubi (8/551).

"The verse is a rebuke for the *'Ulamaa* (scholars) in relation to leaving the commanding of the Ma'ruf (lawful) and forbidding the *Munkar* (unlawful)' [38].

"Indeed, by Allah, they are deserving of every rebuke and fitting of every threat (of punishment). That is because the bad scholars are the cause of every corruption and evil and bringers of every trial and discord. So how can the people be rectified and become upright if the scholars are corrupt? Or how can the people be deterred (from acts of disobedience) if the scholars are perpetrators (of them)? Or how can the magnitude of the acts of disobedience to Allah be instilled in the hearts of those who are ignorant, when the scholars in their actions and statements make them appear insignificant? How will they be made to desire obedience (to Allah) whilst the scholars don't comply with it? How will they stop at the limits whilst the scholars transgress them? How would they leave the innovations when the scholars see them and do not condemn them? How would they abstain from the doubtful matters whilst the scholars view them to be good and wholesome and consume freely from them? Indeed, there are areas of the Haram (prohibited) which they don't refuse and areas of piety that they don't approach" [39].

The corruption of the distinguished people of knowledge is an indication of the penetration of corruption and its deep rootedness within societies. The Ma'siyah (act of disobedience to Allah) is a spiritual sickness and its treatment is knowledge. If the treatment is found but the ailment is not lifted, that indicates the deep rootedness of the sickness and its severity [40]. The skilled craft

---

[38] Tafsir Al-Qurtubi (6/237).
[39] Tanbeeh Al-Ghaafileen 'An A'amaal Al-Jaahileen, Ibn An-Nuhaas (p 85).
[40] Refer to: Tafsir Ar-Raaziy (12/393).

is greater in magnitude than the work, because it is accomplished after training and deliberation, and leaving the Hisbah (accounting) is greater in magnitude than falling into the act of disobedience. That is because the person takes delight in the act of disobedience, which is not the case with accounting and as such its censure is more emphatic [41].

The reported tradition contains a measure for scholarship. In accordance with the amount of the scholar's effort and striving, in addition to his undertaking of the role of commanding the Ma'ruf and forbidding the *Munkar*, his rank with Allah and his impact among the people are measured. This can be observed in the biographies of the influential and impactful examples who were sources of renewal in the procession of the Ummah as a whole. Their impact extended from the circles of knowledge to the domain of action, from the (learning and teaching) rooms of the Masjid to the alleys of the streets. Their lessons were witnessed and their books were widely disseminated.

This statement

أخوفُ عندي منها

"That is more frightening to me than it" takes hold of the heart of the one who reflects upon how those pure distinguished personalities lived alongside the Qur'an. Their reading of it was not a rushed matter, as regulating the feelings of the heart with the verses of the Qur'an does not occur except after contemplation

---

[41] Refer to: Tafsir Al-Baidaawiy (2/134).

and thinking deeply upon its verses, examining them and living with them [42].

"That we refrain from forbidding!" This piece of guidance informs of a great characteristic (*Khuluq*) from the characteristics (*Akhlaq*) of the scholars, manifested in the examination of the self, humbleness and the admission of shortcomings in respect to the *Haqq* (right) of Allah تعالى. This demonstrates the primary radiances of the verses found within the heart of the one who comprehends, where he acknowledges his own shortcomings and does not attempt to vindicate himself or paint himself as being pure. This admission leads him to seek the forgiveness of Allah تعالى and to repent to Him. The chains are then undone from his heart and the exhortations of the verses radiate within it. The practise of these people (scholars) over time testifies to this. How great was the harm that they were afflicted with it due to their undertaking of accounting by knowledge, action, exhortation, and reminding.

This portion of guidance includes the teaching of those who think deeply upon matters to exemplify the verses related to accounting oneself and presenting the self before the verses of the Qur'an for examination. As such, the Muslim asks himself: Am I from the people mentioned in this verse? Have I complied with its command? Have I abstained from what it has forbidden? This is clear in the reported tradition of Ad-Dahhaak (DoD: 102 AH) in

---

[42] Ibn ul-Atheer said in respect to the Tathweer (examination) of the Qur'an: That it means: To examine it and think deeply in its meanings and explanations (Tafsir). Refer to: An-Nihaayah Fee Ghareb Al-Hadith (1/229) under the root of ث و ر.

respect to presenting himself for examination and measure in light of the verse.

The path towards fulfilling this role from among the roles of the scholars is by: Having *Tawakkul* (reliance) upon Allah, dependence upon His favour and sincerity in the intention towards Him. Al-Ghazaaliy (DoD: 505 AH) said: [This was the way of the scholars and their custom in respect to commanding the *Ma'roof* (good) and forbidding the *Munkar* (evil). That was due to them depending upon the favour of Allah; that He would guard them. And they were content with the judgement of Allah تعالى that He would grant them martyrdom. When they made their intention sincere and pure to Allah, their speech impacted upon the hard hearts] [43].

From that which explains the fear of Ad-Dahhaak (DoD: 102 AH), may Allah's mercy be upon him, from this Ayah, is that abandoning the role and duty of commanding the *Ma'roof* and forbidding the *Munkar* is a sign of the greatest plagues of the scholars. That is reflected in coveting the life of this world (*Dunyaa*) and being attached to it. Concerning this, Al-Imam At-Tabari (DoD: 310 AH) said: In relation to the statement of Allah تعالى:

﴿وَمَا اخْتَلَفَ الَّذِينَ أُوتُوا الْكِتَابَ إِلَّا مِن بَعْدِ مَا جَاءَهُمُ الْعِلْمُ بَغْيًا بَيْنَهُمْ﴾

*"Those who had been given the Scripture did not differ except after the book (knowledge) had come to them, due to **Al-Baghy** (rivalry) among them"*
[TMQ Aali 'Imran: 19]

It was related about Ibn 'Umar, may Allah be pleased with them both:

---

[43] Ihyaa' 'Uloom ud-Deen, Al-Ghazaaliy (2/357).

أنه كان يكثر تلاوة هذه الآية يقول: بغيًا على الدنيا، وطلب ملكها وسلطانها، من

قبلها والله أوتينا، ما كان علينا من يكون، بعد أن يأخذ فينا كتاب الله وسنة نبيه،

ولكنا أوتينا من قبلها

That he used to recite this verse often and say: Rivalry over the *Dunyaa* (life of this world), seeking its dominion and authority through it (i.e. the *Dunyaa*). By Allah we were provided what we were meant to, after taking upon us the Book of Allah and the Sunnah of His Messenger. However, we were given from it (the *Dunyaa*) [44].

This disastrous disease which uproots knowledge from the heart and takes away its splendour has been mentioned by the *Salaf* (righteous predecessors). 'Umar said to Ka'b:

ما يذهب العلم من قلوب العلماء بعد أن حفظوه ووعوه؟ فقال: يذهبه الطمع وتطلب

الحاجات إلى الناس

"What takes away the knowledge from the hearts of the scholars after they memorised it and understood it?" He said: "Covetousness (greed) and constant seeking of things from the people takes it away" [45]

This is the cause of the people's contempt for the scholars and Ibn 'Abbas, may Allah be pleased with them both, spoke the truth when he said:

---

[44] Tafsir At-Tabari (5/283).
[45] Jaami' Bayaan Al-'Ilm Wa Fadlihi, Ibn Abdul Barr (1/693).

لو أن حملة العلم أخذوه بحقه وما ينبغي لأحبهم الله وملائكته والصالحون ولهابهم
الناس، ولكن طلبوا به الدنيا فأبغضهم الله وهانوا على الناس

"If those possessing knowledge take hold of it according to its right and what is appropriate in respect to it, Allah, His Angels and the righteous would love them and the people would greatly respect them. However, if they sought the *Dunyaa* through it (i.e. the knowledge), then Allah would detest them and the people would hold them in contempt" [46]

As the *'Ulamaa* (scholars) and the *'Du'aat* (those who carried the invitation to Islam) were from the people of reformation within the society, as they are like the engraving upon clay and the shadow of the staff. How can the clay be engraved by that which has nothing to engrave within it and when will the shadow become straight if the staff or rod is crooked?![47]. The *Islaah* (reformation) of the people through their reformation is the meaning for the sake of which the Qur'an provided extraordinary care and attention. That is because their impact upon the people cannot be denied. Rabee'ah bin Abi Abdur Rahman (DoD: 136), may Allah's mercy be upon him, said:

الناس عند علمائهم كالصبيان في حجور أمهاتهم، ما نهوهم عنه انتهوا وما أمروهم
به ائتمروا

"The people in relation to their *'Ulamaa* (scholars) are like boys in respect to the prohibitions of their mothers. Whatever they forbid

---

[46] Jaami' Bayaan Al-'Ilm Wa Fadlihi, Ibn Abdul Barr (1/695).
[47] Refer to: Iyhaa' 'Uloom ud-Deen, Al-Ghazaaliy (1/58).

them from, they abstain from (that) and what they command them (to do), they carry it out"[48].

And they are

كمثل النجوم التي يهتدى بها، والأعلام التي يقتدى بها، فإذا تغيبت تحيروا وإذا تركوها ضلوا

"Like the stars through which one is guided by and the signs by which one is led, so, if they were to be absent, they (the people) would be in a state of confusion, and if they abandoned them, they would go astray"[49].

As a natural result of the care and attention that the Qur'an provided to *Islaah* (reformation and correction), the *Salaf* (predecessors) were concerned with the *Islaah* of themselves. This is like the reported tradition which At-Tabari (DoD: 310) attributed to Abu Ad-Dardaa', may Allah be pleased with him, in relation to the *Qawl* of Allah تعالى:

﴿وَعُلِّمْتُم مَّا لَمْ تَعْلَمُوا أَنتُمْ وَلَا آبَاؤُكُمْ﴾

"And you were taught that which neither you nor your fathers knew"

[TMQ Al-An'am: 91]

He said:

إن مِن أكثرِ ما أنا مُخاصَمٌ به غدًا، أن يُقَال: يا أبا الدرداء! قد علِمْت، فماذا عمِلْتَ فيما علِمْتَ؟!

---

[48] Jaami' Bayaan Al-'Ilm Wa Fadlihi, Ibn Abdul Barr (2/988).

[49] Hulyat Al-*Awliyaa'*, Abu Nu'aim (2/283).

From that which I will be most disputed against tomorrow, is that it will be said: O Abu Ad-Dardaa'! You knew, so what have you done in respect to what you knew?! [50]

Here, he illustrates the greatest secret for attaining benefit through the action. That is to act with knowledge by which the person benefits himself and then the Ummah benefits through his knowledge. That is like what Ibn Al-Jawziy (DoD: 597 AH) said concerning his *Mashaayikh* (Scholar teachers):

لقيتُ مشايخ أحوالهم مختلفة، يتفاوتون في مقاديرهم في العلم، وكان أنفعهم لي في صحبته العامل منهم بعلمه، وإن كان غيره أعلم منه

I have met Mashaayikh whose circumstances differed. There was a disparity in their abilities in respect to knowledge. The one who was most beneficial to me from them in terms of his company was the one from them who acted by his knowledge, even if other than him was more knowledgeable than him] [51].

Through knowledge ('*Ilm*) and action ('*Amal*) the model examples arise, and others are brought low. Just as there is salvation for the world in acting with knowledge, the soundness and uprightness of the Ummah also relies upon that combination.

The soundness and uprightness of the model examples within the society has the greatest impact upon its individuals and building its future. If you have seen a productive, successful and upright society, then know that behind that there are men to be seen who are like the ears (or spikes) of corn in terms of giving (in abundance) and like suns illuminating (their surroundings). O

---

[50] Tafsir At-Tabari (9/395).
[51] Said Al-Khaatir, Ibn ul-Jawziy (p 158).

Allah, what gratitude belongs to you! In the model examples when they become upright!

The Exhortation of the Distinguished Personalities

Al-Imam At-Tabari (DoD: 310) attributed the following statement to 'Umar bin Al-Khattab, may Allah be pleased with him, in relation to His *Qawl* تعالى:

﴿وَمَن يُرِدْ أَن يُضِلَّهُ يَجْعَلْ صَدْرَهُ ضَيِّقًا حَرَجًا﴾

"And whoever He wants to misguide, He makes his breast tight and constricted (Harajan)"   [TMQ Al-An'am: 125]

ابغوني رجلًا من كِنانة واجعلوه راعيًا، ولْيَكُنْ مُدْلِجِيًّا، فأَتَوْه به، فقال له عمر: يا فتى ما الحَرَجة؟ قال: الحَرَجة فينا الشجرةُ تكونُ بينَ الأشجارِ التي لا تصل إليها راعية، ولا وَحْشِيَّة، ولا شيءٌ! فقال عمر: كذلك قلب المنافق، لا يصل إليه شيءٌ من الخير!

That he, may Allah be pleased with him, said: "Seek a man from Kinaanah for me and make sure he is a shepherd, and let him be Mudlaji (from the Mudlaj tribe of Kinaanah). They brought him and 'Umar then asked him: "O young man, what is Al-*Harajah*?" He answered: "The *Harajah*, as we know it, is a tree that is among trees which no herdswoman, no (female) wild animal and nothing can reach!" 'Umar then said: "That is like the heart of the hypocrite, nothing of goodness reaches it!" [52]

'Umar would not have been able to have extracted this exhorting guidance: "That is like the heart of the hypocrite, nothing of

---

[52] Tafsir At-Tabari (9/544).

goodness reaches it" had it not been for the *Tawfeeq* of Allah تعالى, accompanied by an examination of the points of guidance contained in this verse and its radiances, in addition to his good approach In respect to instructing and teaching the people. The beginning of this reported tradition contains a fascinating and stirring instruction whilst its end contains an impactful exhortation, whilst 'Umar, may Allah be pleased with him, was inspired in exhortation and knowledge. How could that not be the case when Ibn Mas'ud, may Allah be pleased with him, said about him:

لقد أحببتُ عمر حبًّا حتى لقد خفت الله، لو أني أعلمُ أن كلبًا يحبه عمر لأحببته، ولوددتُ أني كنتُ خادمًا لعمر حتى أموت، ولقد وجد فقده كل شيء حتى العِضَاه، إن إسلامه كان فتحًا، وإن هجرته كانت نصرًا، وإن سلطانه كان رحمة

I loved 'Umar to the extent that I feared Allah. If I had known of a dog that 'Umar loved I would have loved it and I wished that I would serve 'Umar until my death. Everything felt his passing and even the trees with large thorns. Indeed, his Islam was a conquest, his migration (Hijrah) a victory and his authority (or rule) a mercy [53].

The reported tradition demonstrates the genius qualities of 'Umar, may Allah be pleased with him, in respect to teaching and exhortation. It was not only guidance which 'Umar dispersed but rather he wrapped it with teaching and exhortation employing an

---

[53] Recorded by Al-Imam Ahmad in relation to the Fadaa'il (virtues of) As-Sahaabah (1/247).

influential and impactful style among those present. It was therefore knowledge and education, and this was the nature of the Rabbaaniyeen (people of *Taqwaa* and obedience to Allah who followed His guidance) who act in accordance with the Book (Al-Qur'an) and study it.

Concerning his statement:

ابغوني رجلًا من كِنانة واجعلوه راعيًا، ولْيَكُنْ مُدْلِجِيًّا

"Seek a man from Kinaanah for me and make sure he is a shepherd, and let him be Mudlaji (from the Mudlaj tribe of Kinaanah)".

This conditional introduction represents education and instruction for the Ummah in respect to referring to the people of expertise. That is because those Arabs were people of language and natural disposition, and it was upon their dialect and language that the Qur'an descended.

The characteristics of genius found in this reported tradition include the application of the pillars of *At-Tadabbur* (deep thinking and contemplation). The first pillar is the sound understanding of the verse which was accomplished through 'Umar's examination of the meaning of the verse in accordance with the Arabic language as an education for the Ummah concerning the necessity of examining the unclear verses of the Qur'an from its correct sources. Then comes the second pillar which relates to what this understanding dictates in respect to the one who wants to consider and act. He said:

وكذلك قلب المنافق لا يصل إليه شيء من الخير

"That is like the heart of the hypocrite, nothing of goodness reaches it!".

It reflects an impactful style for the one present at this scene. That is because when he informed them of the meaning of the *"Harajah"*, and they consequently visualised its reality, that exhortative message came for the believers in relation to paying attention to and taking care of the purity of the heart and warning about the misguidance of the heart. That is so that it would not become like this tree in terms of being tightened and constricted and unable to attain benefit from the verses of the Qur'an and its exhortations.

O blessed one, within this reported tradition (of 'Umar) you will find the coming together of the foundations of sound exhortation:

1 - That it has been taken from the Qur'an Al-Karim, in the case where the whole of the Qur'an is an exhortation (*Maw'izhah*):

﴿يَا أَيُّهَا النَّاسُ قَدْ جَاءَتْكُم مَّوْعِظَةٌ مِّن رَّبِّكُمْ وَشِفَاءٌ لِّمَا فِي الصُّدُورِ وَهُدًى وَرَحْمَةٌ لِّلْمُؤْمِنِينَ﴾

"O mankind, there has to come to you a good exhortation (Maw'izhah) from your Lord and healing for what is in the breasts and a guidance and a mercy for the believers"   [TMQ Yunus: 57]

2 - It is based upon study, knowledge and asking the people of expertise or specialists. That is in accordance with His *Qawl* تعالى:

﴿فَاسْأَلْ بِهِ خَبِيرًا﴾

"So, ask one who is well informed about Him"   [TMQ Al-Furqan: 59]

3 - It contains exhortation by way of example (or similitude) and it is this style which has the greatest impact and effect. This has come demonstrated in numerous Ahadeeth including the Hadith

of Abu Musa Al-Ash'ariy, may Allah be pleased with him, from the Nabi ﷺ who said:

إِنَّ مَثَلَ مَا بَعَثَنِي اللَّهُ بِهِ عَزَّ وَجَلَّ مِنَ الْهُدَى وَالْعِلْمِ كَمَثَلِ غَيْثٍ أَصَابَ أَرْضًا فَكَانَتْ مِنْهَا طَائِفَةٌ طَيِّبَةٌ قَبِلَتِ الْمَاءَ فَأَنْبَتَتِ الْكَلَأَ وَالْعُشْبَ الْكَثِيرَ وَكَانَ مِنْهَا أَجَادِبُ أَمْسَكَتِ الْمَاءَ فَنَفَعَ اللَّهُ بِهَا النَّاسَ فَشَرِبُوا مِنْهَا وَسَقَوْا وَرَعَوْا وَأَصَابَ طَائِفَةً مِنْهَا أُخْرَى إِنَّمَا هِيَ قِيعَانٌ لَا تُمْسِكُ مَاءً وَلَا تُنْبِتُ كَلَأً فَذَلِكَ مَثَلُ مَنْ فَقُهَ فِي دِينِ اللَّهِ وَنَفَعَهُ بِمَا بَعَثَنِي اللَّهُ بِهِ فَعَلِمَ وَعَلَّمَ وَمَثَلُ مَنْ لَمْ يَرْفَعْ بِذَلِكَ رَأْسًا وَلَمْ يَقْبَلْ هُدَى اللَّهِ الَّذِي أُرْسِلْتُ بِهِ

The similitude of that guidance and knowledge with which Allah, the Exalted and Glorious, has sent me is that of rain falling upon the earth. There is a good piece of land which receives the rainfall (eagerly) and as a result herbage and grass grows abundantly. Then there is a land hard and barren which retains water and the people derive benefit from it, so, they drink from it, make the animals drink from it and graze with it. Then there is another land which is barren. Neither water is retained in it, nor does grass grow in it. And that (i.e. the first and second examples) is the similitude of the one who acquires understanding in the *Deen* of Allah and he is benefited by what Allah sent me with, so, he learns and teaches (others). And (the second is) the example of the one who does not pay heed to (the revealed knowledge) and thus does not accept guidance of Allah with which I have been sent" [54].

---

[54] Recorded by Al-Bukhari, Kitaab ul-'Ilm, Chapter: Fadl Min 'Ilm (Virtue from knowledge), Hadith number: (79).

This scene of the reported tradition (of 'Umar) contains within it a message for male and female teachers and *'Du'aat* (inviters to the Islamic message) for them to pay close attention to exhorting the hearts through the verses of the Qur'an Al Karim. The Qur'an, its verses and exhortations contain a remarkable force upon the inner selves. If you were to have searched for the best stories, parables or statements, you would never have found the perfect precedence except within this Qur'an Al-Azheem. Allah spoke the truth and who is more truthful than Allah in speech:

﴿وَلَوْ أَنَّ قُرْآنًا سُيِّرَتْ بِهِ الْجِبَالُ أَوْ قُطِّعَتْ بِهِ الْأَرْضُ أَوْ كُلِّمَ بِهِ الْمَوْتَىٰ ۚ بَل لِّلَّهِ الْأَمْرُ جَمِيعًا ۗ أَفَلَمْ يَيْأَسِ الَّذِينَ آمَنُوا أَن لَّوْ يَشَاءُ اللَّهُ لَهَدَى النَّاسَ جَمِيعًا﴾

"And if there was any Qur'an by which the mountains would be removed or the earth would be broken apart or the dead would be made to speak, [it would be this Qur'an], but to Allah belongs the affair entirely. Then have those who believed not accepted that had Allah willed, He would have guided the people, all of them?" [TMQ Ar-Ra'd: 31]

The Pure Heart and the Hidden (or secret) Voice

Al-Imam At-Tabari (DoD: 310 AH) attributed to Al-Hasan Al-Basriy (DoD: 110 AH), in relation to His *Qawl* تعالى:

﴿ادْعُوا رَبَّكُمْ تَضَرُّعًا وَخُفْيَةً﴾

"Call upon your Lord in humility and privately"

[TMQ Al-A'raaf: 55]

That he said:

إن كان الرجلُ لقد جَمَعَ القرآنَ وما يشعُرُ جارُه، وإن كان الرجلُ لقد فَقِهَ الفقهَ الكثيرَ وما يشعُرُ به الناس، وإن كان الرجلُ لِيُصَلِّي الصلاةَ الطويلةَ في بيتِه، وعندَه الزَّوْرُ[55] وما يَشْعرون به، ولقد أدركنا أقوامًا ما كان على الأرضِ من عملٍ يقْدِرون على أن يعْمَلوه في السرِّ فيكون علانيةً أبدًا، ولقد كان المسلمون يجتهدون في الدعاء، وما يُسْمَع لهم صوت، إن كان إلا هَمْسًا بينهم وبين ربهم، وذلك أن الله يقول

There is the man who accumulated the Qur'an whilst his neighbour was unaware of that. There is the man who learned and understood a great deal of *Fiqh* whilst the people were unaware of that. There was the man who used to pray lengthy prayers in his house whilst he had visitors and yet they were unaware of that. We have come across peoples where there was no action upon the earth that they were able to do in secret and as such it would always be open (or in public). The Muslims used to strive and exert themselves in the *Du'aa* (supplication) and not a sound would be heard from them, in the case where it was only a whisper between them and their *Rabb* (Lord). That is as Allah says:

$$﴿ادْعُوا رَبَّكُمْ تَضَرُّعًا وَخُفْيَةً﴾$$

"Call upon your Lord in humility and privately"   [TMQ Al-A'raaf: 55]

And that is because Allah mentioned a righteous slave, was pleased with his action and then said:

$$﴿إِذْ نَادَىٰ رَبَّهُ نِدَاءً خَفِيًّا﴾$$

"When he called to his Lord a private supplication (Maryam: 3)" [56]

These are not mere tales but rather Quranic beacons of light that illustrate models to comply practically with the Quran in life and to pour sincerity into the blood of life. Sincerity would become the symbol of life and not merely a tweet or meeting which is then tarnished by the infatuation of self-portrayal and vainglory.

In the circles of the Qur'an and Dhikr (making remembrance of Allah) you truly find *Ikhlaas* (sincerity):

$$إن كان الرجلُ لقد جَمَعَ القرآنَ وما يشعُرُ جارُه$$

"There is the man who accumulated the Qur'an whilst his neighbour was unaware of that".

In the seeking of knowledge sincerity is present:

---

[56] Tafsir At-Tabari (10/248).

وإنْ كان الرجلُ لقد فَقِهَ الفقهَ الكثيرَ وما يشعُرُ به الناس

"There is the man who learned and understood a great deal of *Fiqh* whilst the people were unaware of that",

and sincerity is present when there are visitors:

وإنْ كان الرجلُ لِيُصَلِّي الصلاةَ الطويلةَ في بيتِه، وعندَه الزَّوْر وما يَشْعرون به

"There was the man who used to pray lengthy prayers in his house whilst he had visitors and yet they were unaware of that".

This reflects a Quranic observance in the shade of this verse despite mentioning the *Du'aa* (supplication) alone. However, it represents the splendour of analogy when it transforms to the *Fiqh* (understanding) of life and not just issues or areas of knowledge. The sound analogy is one of the methodological characteristics of the *Salaf* in respect to the *Tadabbur* (deep thinking and contemplation upon the Qur'an). That is because the *Sharee'ah* does not differentiate between the matters resembling each other. In this *Tadabbur* (deep thought and contemplation), O blessed one, you read their warm welcoming of the circumstances of the Prophets and righteous.

This reported tradition contains an affirmation of a great principle from among the fundamental principles of the *Sharee'ah*: It is that the secret in respect to that which is not obligatory from the actions of righteousness and obedience are greater in reward than the open [57]. That is because it is greater in terms of severing the route to hypocrisy and insincerity. In addition, its benefits upon the individual are great in respect to building sincerity, the depth

---

[57] Tafseer Ibn Atiyyah (2/410), Tafseer Ibn Hayyan (5/68)

of *Tawakkul* (reliance upon Allah) and rectifying the relationship with Allah تعالى.

When sincerity becomes a way of life, it represents the greatest motive for action and rectifying the self. This is like what was related concerning 'Umar Ibn Abdul 'Azeez (DoD: 101 AH) when one day he was speaking among a group of his brothers. He was engaged in speech and good exhortation when he looked at a man from among his attendees who was shedding tears quickly. He then interrupted his speech and the one relating from him, Maymoon bin Mihraan (DoD: 117 AH) said to him: "Continue O Leader of the believers!". He ('Umar) said: "Hold off! For verily in the speech is a Fitnah (trial) and actions are more becoming of the believer than speech" [58].

The heart attached to Allah is therefore motivated towards tireless devotion to the action of the hereafter. As such, the person does not leave an action except that he engages in another:

$$﴿فَإِذَا فَرَغْتَ فَانصَبْ﴾$$

"So, when you have finished [your duties], then stand up [for worship]"
[TMQ Ash-*Sharh*: 7]

Therefore, nothing detaches him (the believer) from Allah!

As for the heart which is attached to people, then it is disrupted by everything! Is there anything greater to detach one from the path than hypocrisy and seeking fame?!

---

[58] Refer to: Shu'ab ul-Imaan, Al-Bayhaqi (4979), Al-*Ikhlaas*, Ibn Abi Ad-Dunyaa (p 69).

﴿إِنَّ الْمُنَافِقِينَ يُخَادِعُونَ اللَّهَ وَهُوَ خَادِعُهُمْ وَإِذَا قَامُوا إِلَى الصَّلَاةِ قَامُوا كُسَالَىٰ يُرَاءُونَ النَّاسَ وَلَا يَذْكُرُونَ اللَّهَ إِلَّا قَلِيلًا﴾

"Indeed, the hypocrites [think to] deceive Allah, but He is deceiving them. And when they stand for prayer, they stand lazily, showing [themselves to] the people and not remembering Allah except a little"

[TMQ An-Nisaa': 142]

If the needs of the life of this world require concealment, then the needs of the hereafter are more entitled to that. And if we conceal the blessings of the *Dunyaa* (life of this world) out of fear for them from the envious, then the blessings of the hereafter in terms of worshipping and turning to Allah are more deserving of that. For every blessing there is someone envious over it whether it is small or large and there is nothing safer for the one being envied than to conceal his blessing from the eyes of the envious [59].

From among the amazing brilliances of Al-Imaam Ibn Taymiyah (DoD: 728) concerning this subject matter is his statement, may Allah's mercy be upon Him: [And how many people possessing a heart, closeness and condition attached to Allah تعالى spoke about these, informed (others) of them, and then the envious snatched them away from him. **For this reason, the aware and the Shuyookh advised that the secret with Allah تعالى be preserved and that the person should not inform anyone about it.** And concerning the people, then the greatest thing is to conceal their situations (or relationships) with Allah تعالى, what Allah has granted from His love and intimacy to him and the association of the heart. That is especially in respect to his action for the one who is guided and

---

[59] Refer to: Majmoo' Al-Fataawaa, Sheikh ul-Islam Ibn Taymiyah (15/18).

follows the spiritual path. (However) If one of them was to be facilitated and the foundations of that wholesome tree, the basis of which is firm and its branches are in the sky, was strengthened and made firm in his heart, where storms are not feared in respect to it, then if he were to reveal his condition with Allah تعالى so that others are led by him and follow him in that, he should not be concerned! This represents a door to great benefit which only its people (or beneficiaries) are aware of!] [60].

By Allah, O male believer and female believer, strive hard in the intention and to pay utmost care and attention to the private (or secret) actions. That is because they are known to Allah and heard by Him. Al-Imam Qatadah (DoD: 117 AH) spoke the truth when he said:

إن الله يعلم القلب النقي، ويسمع الصوت الخفي

Verily, Allah knows the pure heart and hears the secret (or unseen) voice. [61]

---

[60] Majmoo' Al-Fataawaa, Sheikh ul-Islam Ibn Taymiyah (15/18)

[61] Tafsir At-Tabari (15/453).

The Rain of the Hearts

Just as the rain falls upon the ground, the *Wahy* (revelation) descends upon the heart. If the heart was a wholesome ground, it would receive, be purified by and overflow with goodness. If it was contrary to that, it would be impenetrable and overflow with badness and harm and it would produce thorns and suffering. Its ground would become tough and there will be no benefit in it.

These meanings were acknowledged by the *Salaf* (predecessors) just as was mentioned in the reported tradition of Al-Imam At-Tabari (DoD: 310 AH) attributed to As-Suddiy (DoD: 127 AH), concerning the *Qawl* of Allah تعالى:

﴿وَالْبَلَدُ الطَّيِّبُ يَخْرُجُ نَبَاتُهُ بِإِذْنِ رَبِّهِ ۖ وَالَّذِي خَبُثَ لَا يَخْرُجُ إِلَّا نَكِدًا ﴾

"And the good land, its vegetation comes forth by the permission of its Lord; but that which is bad, brings forth nothing except Nakid (a little that does not benefit)"
[TMQ Al-A'raf: 58]

He said: [An-Nakid means: The thing which is little (or meagre) that does not benefit. The hearts were like that when the Qur'an was revealed. That is because when the Qur'an enters the heart of the believer, he believes in it and *Iman* (belief) becomes firmly established in him. When the Qur'an enters the heart of the disbeliever nothing from it attaches to it that benefits him and nothing of *Iman* is established in him apart from that which does not benefit. Just like this land did not produce except that which does not benefit it in terms of vegetation] [62]

---

[62] Tafsir At-Tabari: 10/259).

Therefore, just as the farmer seeks to rectify his actual ground, As-Suddiy (DoD: 127 AH), may Allah's mercy be upon him, in this reported tradition seeks to guide to the point that the believer is in even greater need to seek to rectify his spiritual ground, for his heart to bear fruit and radiate with the illuminations of the *Wahy* (divine revelation).

Indeed, "The good heart, when the rains of the Qur'an descend upon it, in terms of its restraints and forbiddances, its exhortations and its Halal and Haram, that Qur'an produces fruits in that heart; fruits that are greater than the fruits of the fertile ground when the rain falls upon it. The fruit of *Iman* in Allah تعالى is yielded, the purification from the pollutions of sinful acts and disbelief occurs, and compliance to the command of Allah and the abstention from of all that He has forbidden comes into fruition.

The rain of the Qur'an gives fruit to every good characteristic or quality within the heart of the believer. That is like the fear of Allah تعالى, seeking forgiveness at the time of lapses, repenting sincerely to Him, generosity, courage, contentment with the Qadaa (decree) of Allah تعالى, giving preference to others and not being miserly, among other noble and beautiful Islamic characteristics and qualities" [63].

The reported tradition demonstrates the appropriateness of the choice of this metaphor for the hearts of the sons of Adam. That is because there is resemblance between them and the ground as the ground is their origin and the fundamental element from which they were created. As such, when the rain falls from the sky and

---

[63] Al-'Adhb Al-Nameer, Ash-Shinqeetiy (3/432).

reaches the fertile ground it produces a major impact within it and the crops, grains, fruits, vegetations and green pastures grow and flourish. It then comes to be vividly displayed in garments which have been adorned with varieties of plants and vegetation [64].

The guidance (here) is that the one who contemplates becomes fearful that his heart does not become like the infertile ground which is not benefited by the exhortations of the Qur'an and its restraints. The guidance is also for the one searching for the life of his heart to devote himself to the Qur'an and for those involved in education to take benefit from it in the presentation of examples and to make them easier to comprehend and be visualised by the students. That is because it is a teaching style that has a major impact upon the recipient.

The reported tradition demonstrates how much care and attention the *Salaf* (predecessors) provided to the rectification of the hearts and reflects how they captured the intimations of the Qur'an Al-Karim related to its rectification, in an exhortation indicating that the central point of the matter is the accomplishment of the soundness and well-being of the hearts. As such, exhortation should be devoted to its rectification. Being preoccupied with the rectification of the limbs (i.e. actions) whilst neglecting the soundness and well-being of the heart demonstrates a preoccupation with the means away from the main aims, which reflects a rupture in understanding the path towards Allah تعالى.

Concerning this great verse:

---

[64] Al-'Adhb Al-Nameer, Ash-Shinqeetiy (3/431).

﴿وَالْبَلَدُ الطَّيِّبُ يَخْرُجُ نَبَاتُهُ بِإِذْنِ رَبِّهِۦ وَالَّذِي خَبُثَ لَا يَخْرُجُ إِلَّا نَكِدًا﴾

"And the good land, its vegetation comes forth by the permission of its Lord; but that which is bad, brings forth nothing except Nakid (a little that does not benefit)" [TMQ Al-A'raf: 58]

It contains an indication and instruction for the male and female believers to pay great attention and care to ridding before adorning, to rid the diseases of the hearts before adorning them with the actions of truthfulness and certainty, so that they may elevate and proceed in action. Concerning this, Ibn Battal (DoD: 449 AH) in his *Sharh* (explanation) of Al-Bukhari said: [No one will accept what Allah has revealed in terms of the guidance and *Deen* except the one who prior to that was pure from associating with Allah and doubt. That which accepts knowledge and guidance (meaning: the hearts) are like the ground that is thirsty for that. It then benefits by it, has life and grows.

Similar to that are these hearts which are free of doubt and Shirk (associating partners with Allah) and are thirsty for the guidance and knowledge. When they retain the knowledge, they become alive through it and then they act, giving life to the last breaths of the people who are in need of what the aware hearts were in need of] [65].

Indeed, from the fruits of the tenderness of the heart and its purity is that it will accept knowledge and benefit by it:

[If the heart was tender and gentle its acceptance of knowledge would be easy, simple and would consolidate in it, making it firm and impactful. However, if the heart was hard and harsh its

---

[65] *Sharh* (explanation) of AL-Bukhari, Ibn Battal (1/163).

acceptance of knowledge would be hard and difficult. It is necessary, alongside that, for the heart to be purified, clear and sound so that knowledge can grow in it and produce wholesome fruits] [66].

As such, make a covenant with your heart and rectify what is inside it, to irrigate your inner self (*Nafs*) with the (nourishing) rain of *Iman* and so that your breast is opened to the verses of the Qur'an:

﴿فَمَن يُرِدِ اللَّهُ أَن يَهْدِيَهُ يَشْرَحْ صَدْرَهُ لِلْإِسْلَامِ ۖ وَمَن يُرِدْ أَن يُضِلَّهُ يَجْعَلْ صَدْرَهُ ضَيِّقًا حَرَجًا كَأَنَّمَا يَصَّعَّدُ فِي السَّمَاءِ ۚ كَذَلِكَ يَجْعَلُ اللَّهُ الرِّجْسَ عَلَى الَّذِينَ لَا يُؤْمِنُونَ﴾

"So, whoever Allah wants to guide, He opens his breast to Islam; and whoever He wants to misguide, He makes his breast tight and constricted as though he were climbing into the sky. Thus does Allah place defilement upon those who do not believe" [TMQ Al-An'am: 125]

---

[66] Majmoo' Fataawaa Sheikh ul-Islam Ibn Taymiyah (9/315).

The Companion of every *Bid'ah* (innovation) is Lowly

Building concepts and correcting them is from the aims of the message brought by Muhammad ﷺ. The sun of this message dawned with a divine system or code of concepts chosen by Allah for this Ummah in order to liberate the minds of its children and illuminate them with the guidance of the Qur'an Al-Karim and to nourish them with its distinguishing rays of light.

The Qur'an was revealed with divine concepts which neither humankind nor the Arabs had knowledge of. It then raised them to the paths of human completion and elevated them to the causes of glory and civilisation. **Therefore, building awareness begins with the generation of these concepts.**

The generation of these concepts fortifies the Ummah's values and offers them impregnability. For this reason, the establishment of nations and the level of their power and influence in this world correlates to the level of their care towards these concepts. That is whilst their continuance and life correlates to the extent of the consolidation of these concepts within the society.

From among the greatest correcting concepts in the Qur'an are: **The concept of *Adh-Dhillah* (lowliness), *Al-'Izzah* (honour) and its correct *Mi'yaar* (measure).** *Al-'Izzah* (honour) reflects that goal which every child of Adam strives for whilst *Adh-Dhillah* (lowliness) reflects that lowest point which every human being grieves over. This is applicable in every age and place and in all lands and countries. Indeed, it even extends to the home of the hereafter:

﴿ثُمَّ يَوْمَ الْقِيَامَةِ يُخْزِيهِمْ وَيَقُولُ أَيْنَ شُرَكَائِيَ الَّذِينَ كُنتُمْ تُشَاقُّونَ فِيهِمْ ۚ قَالَ الَّذِينَ أُوتُوا الْعِلْمَ إِنَّ الْخِزْيَ الْيَوْمَ وَالسُّوءَ عَلَى الْكَافِرِينَ﴾

"Then on the Day of Resurrection He will disgrace them and say: "Where are My 'partners' for whom you used to oppose [the believers]?" Those who were given knowledge will say: "Indeed disgrace, this Day, and misery are upon the disbelievers"	[TMQ An-Nahl: 27]

The mind enlightened with the guidance of the Qur'an notices that this lowliness was ordained by Allah upon His enemies in the *Dunyaa* (life of this world) before the *Aakhirah* (hereafter). Allah تعالى says:

﴿إِنَّ الَّذِينَ اتَّخَذُوا الْعِجْلَ سَيَنَالُهُمْ غَضَبٌ مِّن رَّبِّهِمْ وَذِلَّةٌ فِي الْحَيَاةِ الدُّنْيَا ۚ وَكَذَٰلِكَ نَجْزِي الْمُفْتَرِينَ﴾

"Certainly, those who took the calf (for worship), will be taken by the anger of their Lord and by humiliation (lowliness) in the life of this world. Thus, do We recompense those who invent lies"	[TMQ Al-A'raf: 152]

And He تعالى said in relation to the Ahl ul-*Kitab* (people of the book):

﴿ضُرِبَتْ عَلَيْهِمُ الذِّلَّةُ أَيْنَ مَا ثُقِفُوا إِلَّا بِحَبْلٍ مِّنَ اللَّهِ وَحَبْلٍ مِّنَ النَّاسِ وَبَاءُوا بِغَضَبٍ مِّنَ اللَّهِ وَضُرِبَتْ عَلَيْهِمُ الْمَسْكَنَةُ ۚ ذَٰلِكَ بِأَنَّهُمْ كَانُوا يَكْفُرُونَ بِآيَاتِ اللَّهِ وَيَقْتُلُونَ الْأَنبِيَاءَ بِغَيْرِ حَقٍّ ۚ ذَٰلِكَ بِمَا عَصَوا وَّكَانُوا يَعْتَدُونَ﴾

"Indignity (lowliness) is put over them wherever they may be, except when under a covenant (of protection) from Allah, and from men; they have drawn on themselves the Wrath of Allah, and destruction is put over them. This is because they disbelieved in the Ayat (proofs, evidences,

verses) of Allah and killed the Prophets without right. This is because they disobeyed (Allah) and used to transgress beyond bounds"

[TMQ Aali 'Imran: 112]

Therefore, O blessed one, you will find within the speech about the people of the two books an attestation of the concept of Adh-Dhillah (lowliness) and an affirmation of its precise measure, in that it reflects a divine punishment for those who invent falsehoods in his *Deen*. Lowliness is therefore not something that is connected to a particular occupation, race or colour! The justice of Allah rejects that. Rather, lowliness and indignity are only for the enemies of Allah who oppose His *Deen* and those who invent and fabricate against His *Shar'a* (revealed law):

﴾إِنَّ الَّذِينَ يَفْتَرُونَ عَلَى اللَّهِ الْكَذِبَ لَا يُفْلِحُونَ *مَتَاعٌ قَلِيلٌ وَلَهُمْ عَذَابٌ أَلِيمٌ﴿

"Verily, those who invent lies against Allah will never be successful. (it is only) A brief passing enjoyment (for them), but they will have a painful torment" [TMQ An-Nahl: 116-117]

The inventing of lies and fabrications against Allah has many forms and examples, the greatest of which is the innovation in respect to the *Deen* of Allah and to introduce something within it that is not from it.

It has been reported from Al-Imam Sufyan bin 'Uyainah (DoD: 198 AH), may Allah's mercy be upon him, as related by Al-Imam At-Tabari (DoD: 310 AH) in his Tafsir, that he said concerning the *Qawl* of Allah تعالى:

﴾إِنَّ الَّذِينَ اتَّخَذُوا الْعِجْلَ سَيَنَالُهُمْ غَضَبٌ مِّن رَّبِّهِمْ وَذِلَّةٌ فِي الْحَيَاةِ الدُّنْيَا ۚ وَكَذَلِكَ نَجْزِي الْمُفْتَرِينَ﴿

"Certainly, those who took the calf (for worship), will be taken by the anger of their Lord and by humiliation (lowliness) in the life of this world. Thus, do We recompense those who invent lies"   [TMQ Al-A'raf: 152]

كلُّ صاحبِ بدعةٍ ذليل!

"The Companion of every *Bid'ah* (innovation) is Lowly (*Dhaleel*)!"[67]

This concept reflects a sharp understanding of the context of the verse combined with a deep reading of human history.

This concept was abundantly present among almost the entirety of the *Salaf* (predecessors). Ayub As-Sakhtayaniy (DoD: 131 AH) said: "Abu Qilabah recited this verse:

﴿إِنَّ الَّذِينَ اتَّخَذُوا الْعِجْلَ سَيَنَالُهُمْ غَضَبٌ مِّن رَّبِّهِمْ وَذِلَّةٌ فِي الْحَيَاةِ الدُّنْيَا ۚ وَكَذَٰلِكَ نَجْزِي الْمُفْتَرِينَ﴾

"Certainly, those who took the calf (for worship), will be taken by the anger of their Lord and by humiliation (lowliness) in the life of this world. Thus, do We recompense those who invent lies"   [TMQ Al-A'raf: 152]

And said: "This is the recompense for every inventor of lies and fabricator until the Day of Judgement, that Allah will disgrace him!"[68]

Al-Imam Malik bin Anas (DoD: 179 AH), may Allah's mercy be upon him said:

ما من مبتدع إلا وتجد فوق رأسه ذلة!

---

[67] Tafsir At-Tabari (10/465).
[68] Tafsir At-Tabari (3/565).

"There is no innovator except that you find above his head lowliness (or disgrace)!" [69]

And prior to him, Al-Hasan Al-Basri (DoD: 110 AH), may Allah's mercy be upon, said:

إنَّ ذُلَّ البدعة على أكتافهم، وإن هملجت بهم البَغْلَاتُ، وطقطقت بهم البَرَاذِينُ

"The *Dhullah* (disgrace) of the *Bid'ah* (innovation) will weigh on their shoulders even if they were to gallop on their mules or trot on their work horses" [70]

"Even if they were to gallop on their mules or trot on their work horses". This profound image reflects the greatest affirmation of the lowliness and disgrace being linked to the *Bid'ah* (innovation). And even if they live in palaces in our current time, build skyscrapers and fly in the sky. None of that will erase the lowliness and disgrace from their faces as the *Haqq* (truth) is not cancelled by progression, just as it does not change with the changing of the time and place.

Concerning the invention in His statement تعالى:

﴿وَكَذَلِكَ نَجْزِي الْمُفْتَرِينَ﴾

"Thus, do We recompense those who invent lies"　　　　[TMQ Al-A'raf: 152]

This means invention in the foundations of the *Deen*, by placing (or inventing) beliefs not based on authentic evidence from that which the revelation has guided to. The Prophet of Allah Musa (عليه

---

[69] Tafsir Ath-Tha'labi (4/287).
[70] Tafsir Ibn Kathir (3/478).

السلام) warned his people about worshipping the idols. Allah informed about what took place before this verse when He تعالى said:

﴿وَجَاوَزْنَا بِبَنِي إِسْرَائِيلَ الْبَحْرَ فَأَتَوْا عَلَىٰ قَوْمٍ يَعْكُفُونَ عَلَىٰ أَصْنَامٍ لَّهُمْ﴾

"And We took the Children of Israel across the sea; then they came upon a people devoted to [some] idols of theirs" [TMQ Al-A'raf: 138]

Allah made the recompense for the invention: Anger and disgrace. That was if they were to engage in something like that after the exhortation from Allah تعالى had come to them. It is for that reason that the Arab *Mushrikeen* (polytheists) had not been disgraced and lowly. Then when Muhammad ﷺ came, exhorted and reminded them and established the proof of Allah over them, and then they continued upon their invention, Allah punished them with disgrace and lowliness whilst admiration for them was removed from the hearts of the Arabs and their homelands were taken from them. Then (after that), when those from among them embraced Islam, they attained honour through Islam. [71]

For the one who thinks and contemplates over the context of the ayaat, he will appreciate what Sufyan Bin 'Uyaynah said:

كلُّ صاحبِ بدعةٍ ذليل

"Every Companion of *Bid'ah* (innovation) is Lowly (Dhaleel)!".

That lowliness and ignominy covers every person of *Bid'ah* (innovation) who invents in the *Deen* of Allah and its *Shar'a* (Legislative law) that which is not from it. His wonderful reasoning for this came mentioned in another place where he stated:

---

[71] Refer to: Tafsir Ibn 'Aashour (9/120).

"There is no person of *Bid'ah* (innovation) on the earth except that he finds that lowliness (or disgrace) covers him, and that is (stated) in the Book of Allah!" They asked: Where is it mentioned?" He said: "Have you not heard His statement?":

$$﴿إِنَّ الَّذِينَ اتَّخَذُوا الْعِجْلَ ... ﴾$$

"Certainly, those who took the calf (for worship) ... until the end of the Ayah" [TMQ Al-A'raf: 152]

They said: "O Abu Muhammad, this is specific to the people of the calf!" He said: "No, read what comes after it:

$$﴿وَكَذَلِكَ نَجْزِي الْمُفْتَرِينَ﴾$$

"Thus, do We recompense those who invent lies" [TMQ Al-A'raf: 152]

It applies to every inventor and innovator until the Day of Judgement". [72]

Indeed, Abu Muhammad, may Allah's mercy be upon him, spoke the truth, so how can honour be sought from other than the One who owns it, Glorified and Exalted be He:

$$﴿مَن كَانَ يُرِيدُ الْعِزَّةَ فَلِلَّهِ الْعِزَّةُ جَمِيعًا ۚ إِلَيْهِ يَصْعَدُ الْكَلِمُ الطَّيِّبُ وَالْعَمَلُ الصَّالِحُ يَرْفَعُهُ ۚ وَالَّذِينَ يَمْكُرُونَ السَّيِّئَاتِ لَهُمْ عَذَابٌ شَدِيدٌ ۖ وَمَكْرُ أُولَئِكَ هُوَ يَبُورُ﴾$$

"Whoever desires honour, then to Allah belongs all honour. To Him ascends good speech, and righteous work raises it. But those who plot evil deeds will have a severe punishment and the plotting of those will perish" [TMQ Fatir: 10]

---

[72] Ad-Durr ul-Manthoor, As-Suyooti (3/565).

Rejoice with the Qur'an

When the *Kharaaj* (levy) from Iraq was arriving to the *Amir ul-Mu'mineen* (Leader of the believers) 'Umar bin Al-Khattab, may Allah be pleased with him, he and his servant went out (to meet it). 'Umar then began to count the camels and found (to his surprise) that they were much more than that (i.e. that he thought there would be). 'Umar then began to say: "Al-Hamdu Lillah" (All praise belongs to Allah). His servant then said: "O Leader of the Believers, this, by Allah, is from the Fadl (favor and bounty) of Allah and His mercy". 'Umar replied: "You are lying, this is not it! Allah says:

﴿قُلْ بِفَضْلِ اللَّهِ وَبِرَحْمَتِهِ فَبِذَلِكَ فَلْيَفْرَحُوا هُوَ خَيْرٌ مِّمَّا يَجْمَعُونَ﴾

"Say: "In the Bounty of Allah, and in His Mercy (i.e. Islam and the Qur'an); therein let them rejoice". That is better than what (i.e. the wealth) they amass"
[TMQ Yunus: 58]

And this (i.e. the levy from Iraq) is from that which you amass (of wealth)"] [73]

'Umar, himself, used to be a sheepherder in Makkah, and yet, here on this day, levies of cities and countries were pouring upon him in great quantities! The *Dunyaa* itself in its entirety was coming to 'Umar; however, this would not change 'Umar, may Allah be pleased with him, or alter his principles! What then is the secret behind this firmness of 'Umar when facing the Fitnah (trial and seduction) of wealth, authority, and ruling?! When you read the Tafsir of At-Tabari (DoD: 310 AH) of this verse, you will find

---

[73] Tafsir Ibn Abi Hatim (6/1960).

amazing meanings expressed by the *Salaf* demonstrating to you the characteristics of this firmness.

An example of that is the reported tradition of the scholar of the Ummah Ibn 'Abbas, may Allah be pleased with them both, where he said concerning this verse:

بفضل الله: القرآن، وبرحمته: حين جعلهم من أهل القرآن

"By the Fadl (favor) of Allah (means): Al-Qur'an. By His mercy (means): When he made them from the people of the Qur'an" [74].

Ibn 'Abbas, may Allah be pleased with them both, extracted this guidance from the like of His statement تعالى:

﴿الرَّحْمَٰنُ * عَلَّمَ الْقُرْآنَ﴾

"Ar-Rahman (The Most Beneficent Allah)! (1) Has taught (you mankind) the Quran (by His Mercy)"   [TMQ Ar-Rahman: 1-2]

It reflects a guidance that has been extrapolated from more than one verse.

'Umar spoke the truth, and Ibn 'Abbas spoke the truth; may Allah be pleased with them both. That is because the Qur'an Al-'Azheem is the greatest matter to rejoice in and whoever rejoices in other than it has wronged himself and has placed joy in its wrong place.

If it settles in the heart and facilitates knowledge in it, through its manner of doing so, for its servant and by its mercy to him, accompanied by his understanding and piety with it and his constant beneficence towards it, joy is mandated for him in addition to happiness which is greater than the joy of all that is

---

[74] Tafsir At-Tabari (12/197).

loving and loved equally. He will then continue to be raised in the highest levels of *Iman*, constantly thinking deeply upon its meanings and contemplating its worded expressions, being satisfied with the meanings of the Qur'an and its wisdoms to the exclusion of the speech of people. Then if he comes across something from the sciences of the people, he presents it before the Qur'an and if it testifies to its soundness, he accepts it, otherwise he rejects it, and that is because his ambition and purpose is devoted to what is intended from the speech of his *Rabb* (Lord) [75].

What a great ambition this is and how great an honour this is. Abdur Rahman bin Hasan (DoD: 1285 AH), may Allah's mercy be upon him, said:

وأعلى الهمم وأشرفها: إعظام الرغبة فيما أمر الله به من تدبر القرآن

"And the highest ambitions and the most honorable of them is: Making the desire great in respect to what Allah has commanded in terms of pondering and thinking deeply upon the Qur'an, as He تعالى said:

﴿كِتَابٌ أَنزَلْنَاهُ إِلَيْكَ مُبَارَكٌ لِّيَدَّبَّرُوا آيَاتِهِ وَلِيَتَذَكَّرَ أُولُو الْأَلْبَابِ﴾

"(This is) a Book (the Quran) which We have sent down to you, full of blessings that they may ponder over its Verses, and that men of understanding may be reminded" [TMQ Saad: 29][76]

This praiseworthy joy is praiseworthy in its basis as it reflects joy in the speech of Allah, whilst joy in respect to the speech of Allah

---

[75] Refer: Majmoo' Fataawaa, Sheikh ul-Islam Ibn Taymiyah (16/49-50).
[76] Ad-Durar As-Saniyah Fil Ajwibah An-Najdiyah (11/476).

is a follow-on to the joy in Him تعالى. The believer's joy in his *Rabb* (Lord) is greater than any other source of joy in terms of wealth, ownership, and children. Allah has made the life of the heart based upon *Iman* rest upon this divine joy as its happiness manifests in the heart of *Iman* and its light of beauty manifests in its companion's face. Then the *Dunyaa* (life of this world) will become for him like the condition of the people of Jannah in the case where Allah meets them whilst they are in the light of beauty and happiness[77]. Therefore, the Qur'an, for the believers, represents pleasure and delight that is provided in advance (to that of the hereafter).

This praiseworthy joy is also found in its effects. That is because it is a motive and incentive to acquire knowledge and to increase the understanding of the meanings of the Qur'an. That is as Ad-Dahhak (DoD: 102 AH), may Allah's mercy be upon him, said:

حقٌّ على كل من تعلم الْقُرْآن أَن يكون فَقِيهًا

"It is a right upon everyone who learns the Qur'an to be a *Faqeeh* (someone knowledgeable in the *Sharee'ah* of Islam)][78].

It is also praiseworthy in its fruits for its people as they realize and comprehend the true joy that extends to the hereafter and not that delusional joy that will only be a source of grief and regret in the hereafter.

So be certain O blessed one, that there is nothing more worthy for the slave to be joyful about in this life other than the blessing of the Qur'an and the guidance of Islam. They are two blessings that demand gratitude and praise, contentment and happiness. It is

---

[77] Refer to: Tareeq Al-Hijrataini, Ibn ul-Qayyim (p 281).
[78] Tafsir Ibn ul-Mundhir (1/268) and Tafsir Ibn Abi Hatim (2/692).

better than all that people can accumulate of the temporary goods of this world and its embellishments. Constantly ponder upon the radiances of this verse and repeat them often:

﴿قُلْ بِفَضْلِ اللَّهِ وَبِرَحْمَتِهِ فَبِذَلِكَ فَلْيَفْرَحُوا هُوَ خَيْرٌ مِّمَّا يَجْمَعُونَ﴾

"Say: "In the Bounty of Allah, and in His Mercy (i.e. Islam and the Qur'an); therein let them rejoice". That is better than what (i.e. the wealth) they amass"   [TMQ Yunus: 58]

The Harbour of Safety

He cast them both in the perishing wilderness in a valley containing no vegetation, and he provided them with a sack containing some dates and a drinking vessel. He then left them in silence and went on his way. She then followed after him saying: "Where are you going whilst leaving us in this barren valley?!" He did not turn to her, and she asked: "Has Allah commanded you to do this!?" He replied: "Yes" and she responded with certainty:

إذن لا يضيعنا

"Then Allah will not cause us to be lost (or perish)".

She then returned. The water then run out and the woman and her baby became thirsty. She looked at him fretfully. She then rushed between the two mountains in great distress and a severe trial until Allah permitted her a way out and relief. The water appeared by way of an everlasting miracle, and she began to scoop the water into her drinking vessel. She then drank and fed her child. The Angel then said to her: "Do not fear perishing (or being lost) for verily this here is the House of Allah, which will be built by this boy and his father, and **verily, Allah does not cause its people to be lost (or to perish)".**

The *Yaqeen* (certainty) in Allah was the provision of this woman, and the *Tawakkul* (reliance) upon him was her water vessel: Her statement: **"Then Allah will not cause us to be lost (or perish)"** radiates *Iman* and *Yaqeen*. Allah remained in her best thoughts (Husn Azh-Zhann) and so He saved her from perishing, elevated her status and immortalized her and her son's memory. He legislated her Sunnah as an 'Ibadah (act of worship) for the worshippers. Ibn 'Abbas, may Allah be pleased with them both, related from the Prophet ﷺ, that he said whilst relating her story: [That is the Sa'y (fast walking) of the people (which they undertake) between them both (i.e. As-Safaa and Al-Marwa)].[79]

The *Salaf* (predecessors) have extrapolated the meanings of this story through deep thinking upon the Qur'an Al-'Azheem. An example of that came in a reported tradition attributed by At-Tabari (DoD: 310 AH) to Qatadah (DoD: 117 AH), concerning His statement تعالى:

﴿فَمَا وَجَدْنَا فِيهَا غَيْرَ بَيْتٍ مِّنَ الْمُسْلِمِينَ﴾

"But We found not there any household of the Muslims except one"
[TMQ Adh-Dhariyat: 36]

He, may Allah's mercy be upon him, said:

لو كان فيها أكثرُ من ذلك لأنجاهم الله؛ لتعلموا أن الإيمان عند الله محفوظٌ لا

ضَيْعَةَ على أهله!

"Had there been more than that, then Allah would have saved them, so that you (all) know that *Iman* with Allah is safeguarded (and protected) and there is no loss that afflicts its people!"[80].

This, as you can see, is a reported tradition with great meaning that touches the hearts and fills them with *Iman* and *Yaqeen* (certainty). It talks about the greatest causes of safety in the *Dunyaa* (life of this world) and the *Akhirah* (hereafter) and it guides

---

[79] Al-Bukhari related the story in *Kitab* Ahadeeth Al-Anbiya', number (3364).
[80] Tafsir At-Tabari (21/532).

to the greatest of the keys of safety: The *Iman* in Allah تعالى: "So that you (all) know that the *Iman* with Allah is safeguarded (and protected) and there is no loss that afflicts its people".

"Allah will never let us be lost (or perish)!": This is a statement that the righteous have successively repeated and it extended across generations. Even the Noble Prophet ﷺ said it and declared it with *Yaqeen* and *Iman* in front of his companions on one occasion:

إِنِّي رِسولُ اللهِ وَلَنْ يُضَيِّعُنِي أَبَداً

"Verily, I am the Messenger of Allah and Allah will never (ever) leave me to be lost!"[81].

The *'Ulamaa* (scholars), may Allah have mercy upon them, said: [The human being, all the while he preserves the *Deen* of Allah, Allah preserves him in his body and preserves him in his wealth, family and in his *Deen*. And this is the most important of matters, that Allah preserves him in his *Deen* and keeps him safe from deviation and misguidance[82].

لا ضَيْعَة على أهله

"And there is no loss that afflicts its people":

That is because they have complete safety in the *Dunyaa* and the *Akhirah*. The *Iman* is the greatest preserver and protector of the *Deen* of Allah and it saves one from the loathsome things and

---

[81] Recorded by Al-Bukhari in *Kitab* (the book of the) Tafsir ul-Qur'an (4844) in the chapter: The statement of Allah: "When they gave their Bai'ah (pledge) to you under the tree" (Al-Fat'h: 18). And Muslim recorded it in *Kitab* (the Book of) Al-Jihad Wa s-Sair, the Chapter of Sulh (treaty of) Al-Hudaibiyah, Hadith number (1785.

[82] Sharh Riyad As-Saaliheen, Ash-Sheikh Muhammad Al-Uthaymeen (1/488).

adversities of the *Dunyaa* and the *Akhirah*. That is just as Allah تعالى said:

﴿الَّذِينَ آمَنُوا وَلَمْ يَلْبِسُوا إِيمَانَهُم بِظُلْمٍ أُولَٰئِكَ لَهُمُ الْأَمْنُ وَهُم مُّهْتَدُونَ﴾

"Those who have believed and did not mix their belief with Zhulm (injustice and transgression), those will have security, and they are the [rightly] guided"   [TMQ Al-An'am: 82]

Indeed, this protection extends as well to encompass the protection of the slave in his feelings. Some of the *Salaf* said: [The 'Aalim (scholar) does not grieve [the blameworthy form of grief]] and some of them said:

من حفظ القرآن مُتِّع بعقله

"Whoever preserves (or memorizes) the Qur'an, is equipped with his mind"[83].

It extends to cover the preservation of the body. Abu At-Tayyib At-Tabari [DoD: 450 AH), may Allah's mercy be upon him, said in this regard:

هذه جوارح حفظناها في الصغر، فحفظها الله علينا في الكبر

"(Concerning) these limbs; we have preserved them in young age and so Allah will preserve them for us in old age"[84].

The most noble of the types of protection: Is Allah's protection of His slave in respect to his *Deen* and his *Iman*. He safeguards it for him in his life from the misguided doubts and the prohibited

---

[83] Tafsir Ibn Rajab Al-Hanbaliy (1/575).

[84] Tafsir Ibn Rajab Al-Hanbaliy (1/575-576).

desires, and He safeguards his *Deen* for him in his death by making him pass away upon *Iman* [85]. This reflects the most radiant preservation and the most hidden kindness, whilst the majority do not seek it.

The key to this safety extends to encompass the societies and towns. Al-Imam At-Tabari (DoD: 310 AH) attributed to Ibn 'Abbas, may Allah be pleased with them both, concerning His *Qawl* (statement) تعالى:

﴿وَمَا كَانَ اللَّهُ لِيُعَذِّبَهُمْ وَأَنتَ فِيهِمْ ۚ وَمَا كَانَ اللَّهُ مُعَذِّبَهُمْ وَهُمْ يَسْتَغْفِرُونَ﴾

"But Allah would not punish them while you, [O Muhammad], are among them, and Allah would not punish them while they are seeking forgiveness"　　　　　　　　　　　　　　[TMQ Al-Anfal: 33]

He said:

كان فيهم أمانان: نبيُّ الله والاستغفار، فذهب النبي وبقِي الاستغفار

"They had two (sources of) security: The Prophet of Allah and seeking forgiveness. Then the Prophet ﷺ passed away and seeking forgiveness remained:

﴿وَمَا لَهُمْ أَلَّا يُعَذِّبَهُمُ اللَّهُ وَهُمْ يَصُدُّونَ عَنِ الْمَسْجِدِ الْحَرَامِ﴾

"But why should Allah not punish them while they obstruct [people] from al-Masjid al- Haram"　　　　　　　　　　　　[TMQ Al-Anfal: 34]

فهذا عذاب الآخرة، وذاك عذاب الدنيا

---

[85] Tafsir Ibn Rajab Al-Hanbaliy (1/2/313).

This refers to the punishment of the *Akhirah* (hereafter) whilst the former refers to the punishment of the *Dunyaa* (life of this world)] [86].

The depth of the *Fiqh* (understanding) of Ibn 'Abbas, may Allah be pleased with them both, and the strength of his deduction from the Qur'an Al-Karim is evident in this related tradition of his. It represents an indication which the Ayah guided to, although its extraction from the Ayah was achieved through sound understanding and correct deduction.

Safety (and security) is the source of fear and apprehension for the human being as life on earth, in the past and future, cannot be fulfilled without it. Nothing indicates this better than the statement of Ibrahim Al-Khaleel to his people during his debate with them:

﴿فَأَيُّ الْفَرِيقَيْنِ أَحَقُّ بِالْأَمْنِ ۖ إِن كُنتُمْ تَعْلَمُونَ﴾

"(So) which of the two parties has more right to be in security? If you but know" [TMQ Al-An'am: 81]

If its importance had not been settled in their hearts and minds, this question would not have held any meaning!

In addition, Allah granted the blessing of safety (and security) to Quraish. He said:

﴿الَّذِي أَطْعَمَهُم مِّن جُوعٍ وَآمَنَهُم مِّنْ خَوْفٍ﴾

"Who has fed them against hunger, and has granted them safety (or security) from fear" [TMQ Quraish: 4]

---

[86] Tafsir At-Tabari (11/150-151).

We also notice how the Qur'an links the safety of the life of this world with the safety of the hereafter and this is a matter which has virtually no existence within all human theories related to safety. It rather reflects the miraculous originalities of the Qur'an.

Ibn 'Abbas, may Allah be pleased with him, was explaining the concept of safety (and security) in the Qur'an Al-Karim to the Ummah. It is the security based upon the *Deen*, which if realized, brings the security of the *Dunyaa* as a consequence. If this safety is salvation from the punishment of extermination in the *Dunyaa*, then all the remaining types of safety (and security) are included in that, like economic, political and social safety (and security) and what is like these, as have been mentioned in other verses.

My dear blessed brother, if you were to contemplate the Noble verse:

$$﴿فَمَا وَجَدْنَا فِيهَا غَيْرَ بَيْتٍ مِّنَ الْمُسْلِمِينَ﴾$$

"But We found not there any household of the Muslims except one"

[TMQ Adh-Dhariyat: 36]

Numerous Quranic radiances would become apparent to you and from them, for example, is what some of the scholars of Tafsir mentioned:

"Indeed, the world is like the human body and the existence of the righteous is like the cold and hot foods. The disbelievers and defiantly disobedient are like harmful poisons which reach within it. If the body is emptied of the beneficial elements whilst the harmful elements remain within it, it perishes. However, if it is emptied of the harmful elements whilst the beneficial elements remain within it, its life will be wholesome and thrive. If both are found within it, then the ruling goes to that which is most dominant, and the same applies to the lands (countries) and the 'Ibaad (slaves or people)" [87]

Allah is Most Knowledgeable of what is Best and Most Suitable for His Creation

From among the matters which perplex the human minds is the blessings of Allah upon His slaves manifested in the provision of death! That is because this trial conceals a bestowed favour. Had it not been for it, living would not have provided pleasure and houses, towns, markets and pathways would become narrow and constrictive:

He rushes to rid the souls of harm

And he draws near to the home which is more honourable

The favour of Allah in death is magnified if life, purification and justice is found within it. That is like the *Hikmah* (wisdom) found in *Al-Qisas* [88] [law of retaliation]. In the *Qisas* is life, even if its apparentness is death. It represents the killing of one so that all the people can live and it also reflects life for the killer as it is a means of purification for him as it provides a life for him in the home of the hereafter [89]. It means life for the blood-relatives from the wrath and rage of revenge, just as it also means life for the hearts. So, glorified be the One whose *Sharee'ah* is elevated far above the contrast that has been legislated by the desires of corrupt minds and limited deficient opinions.

Al-Imam At-Tabari (DoD: 310 AH) recorded in his Tafsir concerning His statement تعالى:

---

[88] Refer to: A'alam Al-Muwaqqi'een, Ibn ul-Qayyim (3/351).

[89] Refer to: Tafsir Ath-Tha'labi (4/371) as he spoke about it in relation to the verse.

$$\text{﴿وَلَكُمْ فِي الْقِصَاصِ حَيَاةٌ﴾}$$

"And there is life for you in Al-Qisas (law of equal retribution)"

[TMQ Al-Baqarah: 179]

That Qatadah (DoD: 117 AH), may Allah's mercy be upon him, said:

جعل الله هذا القصاص حياةً ونكالًا، وعظة لأهل السفه والجهل من الناس، وكم من رجل قد همَّ بداهية لولا مخافة القصاص لوقع بها، ولكنَّ الله حجز بالقصاص بعضهم عن بعض، وما أمر الله بأمر قط إلا وهو أمر صلاح في الدنيا والآخرة، ولا نهى الله عن أمر قط إلا وهو أمر فساد في الدنيا والدين، والله أعلم بالذي يصلح خلقه

"Allah made this *Qisas* a life, a warning (exemplary punishment) and an admonition for the foolish and ignorant people. How many men flirted with a calamity and had it not been due to the fear of the *Qisas*, he would have fallen into it. However, Allah has restrained some of them from others through the *Qisas*. Allah has not commanded any matter at all except that it is a matter that brings wellbeing in the *Dunyaa* (life of this world) and the *Akhirah* (hereafter) and Allah has not forbidden any matter at all except that it is a corrupting matter in the *Dunyaa* and *Akhirah*. And Allah is most aware of what is best and most suitable for His creation" [90].

The above tradition highlights an aspect of the distinguishing features of the Quranic legislation which Qatadah (DoD: 117 AH), may Allah be pleased with him, immersed himself into its meanings. It is by making the *Qisas* (equivalent to) life,

---

[90] Tafsir At-Tabari (3/121).

representing one of the most wonderful explanatory compositions in the Qur'an. The Quranic legislation is blended with the explanatory miracle. The one who ponders finds amazing preciseness within the legislative formation, accompanied by excellence in explanation and beauty in its worded expressions.

Four points will become apparent to the one who ponders the points of originality in this amazing Quranic composition which the Arab proverb

القتل أنفى للقتل

"Killing is the greatest negator of killing" exemplifies:

Firstly: Its inclusion of what was in the first example in terms of meanings.

Secondly: The addition of beautiful meanings like the demonstration of justice for its mentioning of the *Qisas*.

Thirdly: It demonstrates the desired purpose for its mentioning of life.

Fourthly: Summoning the desire and fear for the ruling of Allah by it [91].

The reported tradition of Qatadah (DoD: 117 AH), may Allah's mercy be upon him, also contains an aspect related to *Iman* in its indication to the Islamic legislative principle: *"Jalb ul-MaSaalih Wa Daf'u l-Mafaasid"* (Drawing the benefits and repelling the harmful corruptions). This indication of the legislative principle is equivalent to affirming the *Sharee'ah* branches, from which it is

---

[91] Refer to: An-Nukat Fee 'Ijaaz Al-Qur'an, Ar-Rammaniy (p 77-78). The scholars have expanded in respect to the mention of these angles. From among them is As-Suyootiy in Al-Itqaan. He mentions 20 angles related to that. Refer to: Al-Itqaan (3/186/188).

intended to stir the feelings of *Iman* within the sentiment of the Muslim. Reminding the Muslim of it leads him to surrender to these rulings and to comply with them.

The *Yaqeen* (certainty) of the believer that the *Sharee'ah* in its entirety represents uprightness, as Qatadah (DoD: 117 AH) stated, makes the fulfilment of the legal responsibilities of the *Deen* an honour for the believer as he perceives their perfection, and that the well-being of the *Dunyaa* and the *Akhirah* lies in it. He perceives that most of the people had been led astray from these legal responsibilities and that no one would have been guided to them except the one for whom the sun of the message had radiated and the one who was cognisant of the Qur'an and the *Wahy* (divine revelation).

Al-'Izz bin Abdus Salaam (DoD: 660 AH) said:

كل مأمور به ففيه مصلحة الدارين أو إحداهما، وكل منهي عنه ففيه مفسدة فيهما أو في إحداهما، فما كان من الاكتساب محصلًا لأحسن المصالح فهو أفضل الأعمال، وما كان منها محصلًا لأقبح المفاسد فهو أرذل الأعمال

"Everything that has been commanded contains a *Maslahah* (benefit) in the two Homes (i.e. The home (Dar) of the *Dunyaa* (life of this world) and the home (Dar) of the *Akhirah* (hereafter)) or in one of them. And every forbidden matter contains a Mafsadah (harmful corruption) in them both or in one of them. Therefore, the attainment of that which brings the best of the *MaSaalih* (benefits or interests), represents the best of actions. And whatever brings the most heinous of *Mafaasid* (harmful corruptions), represents the lowest (and most despicable) of actions" [92]

It will become evident for the one who examines the Islamic *Sharee'ah* sources that the general *Maqsad* (purpose or aim) of the legislation is: The preservation of the system of the Ummah and the continuance of its uprightness through the uprightness of the Khalifah over it (i.e. "the human being" who has been entrusted with its preservation). That is through a comprehensive reform encompassing his uprightness and the uprightness of his mind, actions and what exists before him in terms of all that exists in the world that he lives in ... That will only occur through the attainment of the *MaSaalih* and avoidance of the *Mafaasid* [93].

Qatadah (DoD: 117 AH), may Allah's mercy be upon him, used the Quranic term of "*Al-Qisas*" and it is likely that he intended by that to illustrate that this wording indicated the nullification of blood measure vengeance and the nullification of killing a member of the killer's tribe if they don't overtake the killer himself [94].

The reported tradition (of Qatadah) reveals how the *Sharee'ah* honours life which makes the one who contemplates realise the blessing that many people do not realize and that is the blessing of life. The way to realize the blessing of life is the life of the *Rooh* (spirit) which is achieved through the *Tadabbur* (deep thinking upon and contemplation) of the Qur'an. The tradition also makes evident an important distinguishing quality of the Islamic legislation, and that is the mixing of the legislation with the exhortation and stirring of hearts, in a clearly complementary

---

[92] Qawaa'id Al-Ahkam Fee Masaalih Al-Anaam, Al-'Izz bin Abdus Salaam (1/8

[93] Refer to: Maqaasid Ash-*Sharee'ah*, Ibn 'Aashour (3/194-230).

[94] Refer to: Tafsir Ibn 'Aashour (2/145).

manner between the legislations of Islam and the life of the believer's heart. That is because the beauty of the *Sharee'ah* cannot be perceived except by the life of the heart, just as these legislations cannot be approached in the most complete manner unless it is via the life of the heart.

The tradition also makes evident that this *Sharee'ah* came as a mercy for all the 'Ibaad (servants and creation) and that the *Sharee'ah* is not bloodthirsty. That it came to preserve and protect lives which represents one of the five essential matters that the *Sharee'ah* came to safeguard.

From among the radiances of the verse:

﴿وَلَكُمْ فِي الْقِصَاصِ حَيَاةٌ﴾

"And there is life for you in Al-Qisas (law of equal retribution)"

[TMQ Al-Baqarah: 179]

Is what Ibn ul-Qayyim (DoD: 751 AH), may Allah's mercy be upon him, said:

فلولا القصاص لفسد العالم، وأهلك الناس بعضهم بعضًا ابتداءً واستيفاءً، فكأن في القصاص دفعًا لمفسدة التجري على الدماء بالجناية وبالاستيفاء، وقد قالتِ العرب في جاهليتها: «القتل أنفى للقتل» وسفك الدماء يحقن الدماء؛ فلم تغسل النجاسة بالنجاسة، بل الجناية نجاسة والقصاص طهرة، وإذا لم يكن بد من موت القاتل ومن استحق القتل فموته بالسيف أنفع له في عاجلته وآجلته

"If it was not for the *Qisas* the world would have become corrupted and the people would have destroyed themselves in provocative acts and those to exact measure (or vengeance). It is like the *Qisas* is a repellent for the Mafsadah which seeks blood by way of crime and exacting measure (vengeance). The Arabs said in Jahiliyah (pre-Islamic period): "Killing is the greatest negator of killing" and the spilling of blood spares (further) blood. The impurity is not washed by another impurity. Indeed, the crime is an impurity whilst the *Qisas* is a purifier. And if the death of the killer and the one who deserved to be killed was necessary, then his death by the sword is more beneficial for him in both his short and long term" [95].

---

[95] A'alam Al-Muwaqqi'een, Ibn ul-Qayyim (3/350-351).

Securing the Rights

بعثَ موسى بالجلالِ، وبعثَ عيسى بالجمالِ، وبعثَ محمد بالكمالِ

"Musa was sent with *Jalaal* (glory), Isa was sent with *Jamaal* (beauty), and Muhammad was sent with *Kamaal* (completion/perfection)"[96].

This all-encompassing speech was said by Al-Imam Abu Al-'Abbas Ibn Taymiyah (DoD: 728 AH) and he, may Allah's mercy be upon him, was truthful in what he said. That is because the complete perfection of the *Sharee'ah* which Muhammad ﷺ came with is perceived in its branches before its fundamentals and in its details before its complete entireties.

From the beauty of the *Sharee'ah* is its organisation of the rights of the people in relation to what exists between them and it's being established upon firm fundamentals based upon the connection of the *Ibad* (slaves) with their *Rabb*. It linked the giving of Zakah with the establishment of the Salah (prayer) and, as such, manifested the beauty of the legislation with beneficence in respect to the right of the Creator and the right of the creation, (manifesting) glory in beauty, and beneficence in completeness.

Within the radiances of the longest verse in the *Kitab* (book) of Allah some of these features of beauty are clearly manifested. The verse was worthy of being named by some of the scholars "Arjaa Ayah"! (The most hoped for verse). Az-Zarkashi (DoD: 794 AH) said in his **"Al-Burhan"**:

---

[96] Al-Jawab As-Sahih Li-Man Baddala *Deen* Al-Maseeh (5/86).

إنَّ الله تعالى أرشد عباده إلى مصالحهم الدنيوية، حتى انتهت العناية بمصالحهم إلى
أن أمرهم بكتابة الدَّين الكبير والحقير، فبمقتضى ذلك يرجى عفو الله تعالى عنهم؛
لظهور أمر العناية العظيمة بهم حتى في مصلحتهم الحقيرة

"Verily, Allah تعالى has guided His slaves to their worldly interests. The care with their interests even reached the point that He commanded them to write down the negligible and large debt. In accordance to that, the pardon of Allah تعالى is hoped for them due to the existence of the great care which has been extended to them, even in relation to the most negligible of their interests (*MaSaalih*)" [97].

The *Salaf* (predecessors) comprehended the divine aims (Maqaasid) of the legislation and its objectives in the verse related to the debt. Their ingeniousness excelled in relation to the gems of guidance and far-reaching exhortations. Al-Imam At-Tabari (DoD: 310 AH), attributed to Qatadah (DoD: 117 AH), may Allah's mercy be upon him, that he said concerning His *Qawl* تعالى:

﴿وَاسْتَشْهِدُوا شَهِيدَيْنِ مِن رِّجَالِكُمْ فَإِن لَّمْ يَكُونَا رَجُلَيْنِ فَرَجُلٌ وَامْرَأَتَانِ﴾

"And bring to witness two witnesses from among your men. And if there are not two men [available], then a man and two women"

[TMQ Al-Baqarah: 282]

---

[97] Al-Burhan Fee 'Uloom ud-*Deen*, Az-Zarkashi (1/446).

عَلِمَ اللهُ أن ستكونُ حقوق، فأَخَذ لبعضِكم من بعضٍ «الثقة» فخُذوا بثقةِ الله،
فإنه أطوعُ لربّكم، وأدرَكُ لأموالِكم، ولعَمْرِي لئن كان تقيًّا لا يَزِيدُه الكتاب إلا خيرًا،
وإن كان فاجرًا فبالحَرَى أن يُؤَدِّيَ إذا علِم أنَّ عليه شُهودًا

"Allah knew that there would be rights and so he took for some of you from others "the trust of assurance" (الثِّقَة). So, take the trust of Allah (that he has provided), because it is more obedient to your *Rabb* (Lord) and is safer for your wealth (or property). By my years, if a person was conscious (fearing) of and obedient to Allah, the *Kitab* (i.e. Qur'an) will not increase him except in goodness, and if he was corrupt (or sinful) then it is more likely that he will fulfil (what is due upon him) when he knows that there are witnesses over it" [98].

Do you not see, O fortunate one, that his speech, may Allah's mercy be upon him, is like a contemporary legal principle that has been penned with eloquence and wisdom, mixing in it *Fiqh* (understanding) with exhortation, and the means with the aims, in easy language which every thinking person can understand?

From the marvels of this principle are: Explaining that the witnesses and authenticating (documentation), in respect to the transaction, is obedience to Allah سبحانه just as it means the safeguarding of the wealth. In this, he, may Allah's mercy be upon him, elucidates the beauty of the *Sharee'ah* and its magnificence in combining between both the good of the *Dunyaa* (life of this world) and the good of the *Aahkirah* (Hereafter).

---

[98] Tafsir At-Tabari (5/92).

Courtrooms are filled with cases that are a result of the abandonment of this divine instructive guidance, reflecting painful illiteracy that has afflicted the Ummah after it abandoned the *Kitab* of Allah and deep thinking upon its legislative meanings.

How many rights have been lost as a result of abandoning this divine instructive guidance?! Just as a proceeding in accordance with the pleasure of Allah means salvation in the hereafter, it also means the safeguarding of the *Dunyaa* (worldly life) of the people.

He enveloped the beauty of this documented evidence with the depth of his *Fiqh* (understanding), may Allah's mercy be upon him, of the categories of the people and the impulses of the inner selves, explaining that the documentation of the rights and witnesses upon debts represents prudence and that there is no contradiction between *Taqwaa* (consciousness of Allah) and the documentation of rights:

ولعَمْرِي لئن كان تقيًّا لا يَزِيدُه الكتاب إلا خيرًا

"By my years, if a person was conscious (fearing) of and obedient to Allah, the *Kitab* (i.e. Qur'an) will not increase him except in good".

That is the reason for the decline or regression which some were afflicted with in relation to the culture of rights. Illiteracy of rights spread among them, and ignorance regarding documented evidence became widespread. Consequently, the wealth of the orphans was squandered, rights regressed and the *Dunyaa* (worldly life) of the people became corrupted based on the argument that documented evidence is not compatible with trust, whilst being heedless to or ignoring that the trust in Allah and His *Shar'a* (law), manifested in written documentation and witnesses, is greater and more worthy of inclining to than the trust of the people.

From this, we know that the longest verse in the *Kitab* of Allah came related to safeguarding the rights of the people and establishing justice among them, highlighting clearly that the *Sharee'ah* came to make the *Dunyaa* prosperous and make it upright, just as it came to bring the prosperity of the hereafter and striving for it. This came as a complete legislative package, establishing that the feeble-mindedness of the laws of the earth are incapable of comparing with the revealed legislation of the heaven:

﴿وَلَا تَسْأَمُوا أَن تَكْتُبُوهُ صَغِيرًا أَوْ كَبِيرًا إِلَىٰ أَجَلِهِ ۚ ذَٰلِكُمْ أَقْسَطُ عِندَ اللَّهِ وَأَقْوَمُ لِلشَّهَادَةِ وَأَدْنَىٰ أَلَّا تَرْتَابُوا﴾

"And do not be [too] weary to write it, whether it is small or large, for its [specified] term. That is more just in the sight of Allah and stronger as evidence and more likely to prevent doubt between you"

[TMQ Al-Baqarah: 282]

To show you, O you who contemplates, the radiances of the verses of the *Deen* in another form, look at what the scholar of Tafsir Ibn Al-'Arabiy (DoD: 543 AH), may Allah's mercy be upon him, said in his book "Ahkam ul-Qur'an", when he said concerning this Ayah, in an encompassing speech:

هي آية عُظمى في الأحكام، مبينة جملًا من الحلال والحرام، وهي أصل في مسائل البيوع، وكثير من الفروع... ونُقل عن الشَّعْبي [ت: 104]: البيوع ثلاثة: بيع بكتاب وشهود، وبيع برهان، وبيع بأمانة؛ وقرأ هذه الآية؛ وكان ابن عمر إذا باع بنقد أشهد، وإذا باع بنسيئة كتب وأشهد، وكان كأبيه وقافًا عند كتاب الله تعالى، مقتديًا برسول الله

"It is a magnificent verse in relation to the Ahkam (rulings), explaining clauses from the Halal and the Haram, and it represents the origin in relation to the issues of sales (or monetary/trade transactions) and many of the branches ... It was transmitted from Ash-Sha'biy (DoD: 543 AH), may Allah's mercy be upon him, that: *Al-Buyoo'* (sales) are three (categories): The sale by writing and witnesses, the sale of Burhan (proof) and the sale of Al-Amanah (trust). He then recited this Ayah (Al-Baqarah: 282). When Ibn 'Umar used to sell with the currency he would have it witnessed and if he traded with Nasee'ah (by delay) he would have it written and witnessed. He was like his father, standing firmly by the *Kitab* of Allah and emulating the Messenger of Allah ﷺ" [99]

---

[99] Ahkam Al-Qur'an, Ibn ul-'Arabiy (1/327-341).

Heedlessness of the Punishment

Their physical wounds had not yet closed, their swords had not yet been sheathed, and their non-physical wounds as the result of the departure of loved ones, the weight of defeat and pain of the calamity were still fresh. They had lost seventy men from their loved ones, each one of whom was alone was equivalent to an Ummah (nation). However, this is the Sunan (fixed ways and universal laws) of Allah, which are true for everyone, whilst the days vary where some are good, and some are bad:

﴿وَتِلْكَ الْأَيَّامُ نُدَاوِلُهَا بَيْنَ النَّاسِ وَلِيَعْلَمَ اللَّهُ الَّذِينَ آمَنُوا وَيَتَّخِذَ مِنكُمْ شُهَدَاءَ﴾

"And so are the days (good and not so good), We give to men by turns, that Allah may test those who believe, and that He may take martyrs from among you"　　　　　　　　　　　　　　　　　　　　[TMQ Aali 'Imran: 140]

There, upon the slope of mount Uhud the greatest of battles took place and one of the greatest lessons for the greatest of generations upon the face of the earth, for those lessons to then be extended in the memory of the Ummah in respect to what mount Uhud and the graves of the martyrs left behind.

The greatest nations are those which forge a victory from their defeat and loftiness from breaking point. That is because pain is a school and revision is the factory for (making) men. For that reason, the Qur'an eternalized the lessons of "Uhud" so that it remains as a fresh shortcoming in the memory of the Ummah and so that every age and every generation can benefit from it.

We do not find that the Qur'an detailed the battle of Badr as it did the battle of Uhud, and that represents a distinguishing sign for the one who contemplates upon the Qur'an!

The answers to that are found in the contemplations of the *Salaf* (predecessors) upon the verses related to the battle of Uhud and its lessons. That is like the reported tradition which Al-Imam At-Tabari (DoD: 310 AH), may Allah's mercy be upon him, attributed to Al-Hasan Al-Basri (DoD: 110 AH), may Allah's mercy be upon him, who said concerning the *Qawl* of Allah تعالى:

﴿وَلَقَدْ عَفَا عَنكُمْ﴾

"And He has already pardoned you" [TMQ Aali 'Imran: 152]

وَكيف عفا عنهم وقد قُتِل منهم سبعون، وقُتِل عمُّ رسول الله r وكُسِرَت رَبَاعِيَّتُه، وشُجَّ في وجهه؟ قال الله I: قد عفَوْتُ عنكم إذ عصَيتُموني أن لا أكون استَأْصَلْتُكم! هؤلاء مع رسول الله وفي سبيل الله، غِضَابٌ لله، يُقَاتِلونَ أعداءَ الله، نُهُوا عن شيءٍ فضيَّعوه، فواللهِ ما تُرِكُوا حتى غُمُّوا بهذا الغَمِّ، فأفْسَقُ الفاسقين اليوم يتجرَّثم كلَّ كبيرة، ويَرْكَبُ كلَّ داهية، ويسحب عليها ثيابه، ويزعم أن لا بأس عليه، فسوف يَعْلَم!

"How could He have pardoned them whilst seventy of them had been killed, the uncle of the Messenger of Allah ﷺ had been killed, his (the Prophet's) lateral incisors (teeth) had been smashed and his face had been split open? Allah تعالى says: "I have pardoned you when you disobeyed me, as I have not uprooted (or eradicated) you! Those who were with the Messenger of Allah ﷺ and in the way of Allah, angry for the sake of Allah, fighting the enemies of Allah, were forbidden from a matter but they were heedless of it. By Allah, they were not left until they were covered by this grief. The most rebellious of the Fasiqeen (rebelliously disobedient) today takes his fill of every major sin, rides every misfortune and draws his cloak over it. He claims that he will be none the worse by it but he will come to know!" [100]

O distinguished one, you can see how the master of the Tabi'een, may Allah's mercy be upon him, illustrated for us the loftiest methodology within the reading of the battle of Uhud, a reading undertaken by those of high esteem. Uhud was not just a battle that came to an end or a passing incident. Rather, it represents reoccurring lessons and admonitions which continue over time. It is for that reason that the Qur'an focused upon it more than other battles.

Within this reported tradition, we find understanding in respect to applying the greater reality upon the reality of the time and employing it to treat the maladies of the people. This reflects the essence of *Tadabbur* (deep thought and reflection) and the peak of *Fiqh* (understanding). The Qur'an was not revealed except for it to be employed and for lessons and admonitions to be taken from it.

In this revelation, the latter is tied to the former. That is because history repeats itself whilst the Sunan (fixed ways and universal laws) of Allah do not change:

$$﴿فَلَن تَجِدَ لِسُنَّتِ اللَّهِ تَبْدِيلًا ۖ وَلَن تَجِدَ لِسُنَّتِ اللَّهِ تَحْوِيلًا﴾$$

"That is as you will never find for the Sunnah of Allah any change and you will never find for the Sunnah of Allah alteration"   [TMQ Fatir: 43]

It opens wide the eyes of the contemplator to not easily pass over or be heedless of the punishments of Allah, as we find in his reported tradition, may Allah's mercy be upon him, that he says:

---

[100] Tafsir At-Tabari (6/144).

وَكيف عفا عنهم وقد قُتِل منهم سبعون، وقُتِل عمُّ رسول الله وكُسِرَت رَبَاعِيَّتُه،

وشُجَّ في وجهه؟!

"How could He have pardoned them whilst seventy of them had been killed, the uncle of the Messenger of Allah ﷺ had been killed, his (i.e. the Prophet's) lateral incisors (teeth) had been smashed and his face had been split open?".

He wants the believer to be alertly aware of the dire consequences of the acts of disobedience, just like the heart was of the early generations of those who used to repent frequently. That is like Al-Imam Al-Fudail bin 'Iyaad (DoD: 187 AH) when he said:

وإني لأعصي الله فأعرف ذلك في خُلق حماري وخادمي

"I disobey Allah and I am aware of that by the characteristics of my donkey and my servant" [101].

Those alive hearts are alertly aware of the dire consequences of the acts of disobedience and persistence upon them. That is because their calamities and evil effects are not delayed but are diminished. However, the measure (of this) is in the extent of seeing the evil consequences before they become excessive and in seeing the danger before it spreads.

فوالله ما تُرِكُوا حتى غُمُّوا بهذا الغَمّ

"By Allah, they were not left until they were covered by this grief"

This refers to those noble companions who were punished by grief whilst grief represents a forgotten punishment. Our tragedy today

---

[101] Hilyah Al-Awliyah, Abu Nu'aim (8/109).

is that we do not understand the punishments of the acts of disobedience except as calculations, like the decrease of wealth, lives and children.

Here is a precious speech from Ibn ul-Jawziy (DoD: 597 AH), may Allah's mercy be upon him, concerning how rarely the one who persists upon acts of disobedience is aware of this and how seldom most of the people pay attention to it. He says:

وربما رأى العاصي سلامة بدنه وماله، فظنَّ أن لا عقوبة، وغفلته عما عوقب به عقوبة، وقد قال الحكماء: المعصية بعد المعصية عقاب المعصية، والحسنة بعد الحسنة ثواب الحسنة، وربما كان العقاب العاجل معنويًّا، كما قال بعض أحبار بني إسرائيل: **يا رب! كم أعصيك ولا تعاقبني! فقيل له: كم أعاقبك وأنت لا تدري! أليس قد حرمتك حلاوة مناجاتي؟!** فمن تأمَّل هذا الجنس من المعاقبة، وجده بالمرصاد

"Perhaps, the disobedient one views the wellbeing of his body and wealth and consequently believes that there is no punishment. That is whilst his unawareness of what he is being punished with is a punishment. The wise people said: The act of disobedience followed by the act of disobedience is the punishment for the act of disobedience. Similarly, the good act followed by the good act is the reward of the good act. It could be that the immediate punishment is emotional (or non-material). That is like some of the Rabbis of Bani Isra'eel said: **O Lord! How often I disobey you, but you don't punish me! It would be said to such a person: How often (or much) I punish you whilst you are not aware! Have I not**

deprived you of the sweetness of conversing with me?! Whoever reflects upon this type of punishment finds it lying in wait" [102].

That pure generation was punished with grief. We are also inevitably punished; however, our greatest punishment is heedlessness and unawareness concerning what we are being punished with. This represents one of the greatest calamities; unawareness (and heedlessness) concerning the punishments. It leads to: Riding and passing over the misfortunes and committing the major sins. The issue is not that those are not punished and that these good people are punished. Rather, the issue is: That these perceive the punishment, repent and are consequently saved and elevated, whilst those are heedless and unaware of the punishment and persist (in their bad). These are aware of the punishment even if it is minute, whilst those who are not aware, do not repent and do not take heed!

From among the radiances of the reported tradition (Al-Athar), is what 'Umar ibn Abdul 'Aziz (DoD: 101 AH) wrote to one of his governors in a letter that Ash-Sha'biy (DoD: 104) marveled at:

أمَّا بعد: فلا تغترَّ بتأخير عقوبة الله تعالى عنك، وإنما يعجل من يخاف الفوت،

والسلام

"Thereafter ... Do not be deceived by the delay of the punishment of Allah تعالى from you. Only the one who fears that it will be missed hastens, and Salaam" [103]

---

[102] Said ul-Khatir, Ibn ul-Jawziy (p65-66).
[103] Al-Uqoobaat, Ibn Abi Ad-*Dunyaa* (p 168).

The Trustworthy Trader

From the splendor of our *Sharee'ah* and its perfection is that the Mubahaat (permissible acts and things) of this worldly life can be acts that draw closeness to Allah and be rewardable acts of obedience:

وَفِي بُضْعِ أَحَدِكُمْ صَدَقَةٌ

"And in the sexual relations of one of you, there is Sadaqah".

They (the Sahabah) asked: "O Messenger of Allah, is there reward in one of us satisfying his desire?"

He said:

أَرَأَيْتُمْ لَوْ وَضَعَهَا فِي حَرَامٍ أَكَانَ عَلَيْهِ فِيهِ وِزْرٌ؟ فَكَذَلِكَ إِذَا وَضَعَهَا فِي الْحَلَالِ كَانَ لَهُ أجر

"Do you see, if he were to place it (the desire) in Haram he would attain its weight (in sin) for it. So, similarly, if he was to place it in the Halal, he would attain a reward (for it)" [104]

An-Nawawi (DoD: 676 AH), may Allah's mercy be upon him, said: [This contains evidence that the *Mubahaat* (permissible things and acts) become (rewardable) acts of obedience via truthful (sincere) intentions] [105]. This is from the expansiveness of the *Sharee'ah* and

---

[104] Muslim, Book of Zakah, chapter: Explanation that the name of Sadaqah applies upon every kind of *Ma'roof*, Hadith number: (1006), from the Hadith of Abu Dharr.
[105] Sharh An-Nawawi of Muslim (7/92).

its mercy. It is for this reason that the master of scholars Mu'adh bin Jabal, may Allah be pleased with him, said:

فإني أحتسب نومتي كما أحتسب قومتي

"For verily I hope for reward from my sleeping just as I anticipate reward from my standing in prayer" [106]

That is, as the *Sharee'ah* did not come to prevent people from the needs and the basis of their livelihoods, just as it did not come to declare war against the *Dunyaa* (worldly life). Rather, it came to regulate the *Dunyaa*.

As such, the original position regarding the norms of the people is that they are Halal (permissible). The majority of the *Fuqaha'* (Scholars) are upon the view that the original ruling in respect to the financial transactions (*Mu'aamalaat*) is that they are Halal and Mubah (permissible), which demonstrates a clear message that this *Sharee'ah* is not in a war against the *Dunyaa*. Indeed, this principle of *Fiqh* (jurisprudence) represents a clear invitation to scatter through the land and to seek the favour and bounty of Allah تعالى.

This is the understanding that the *Salaf* (predecessors) understood from the verses of the rulings related to the area of transactions. Al-Imam At-Tabari (DoD: 310 AH) attributed to Qatadah (DoD: 117), may Allah's mercy be upon him, that concerning the *Qawl* of Allah تعالى:

---

[106] Al-Bukhari, Book of Maghazi (battles), chapter: The dispatch of Abu Musa and Mu'adh to Yemen, Hadith number: (4341).

$$﴿يَا أَيُّهَا الَّذِينَ آمَنُوا لَا تَأْكُلُوا أَمْوَالَكُم بَيْنَكُم بِالْبَاطِلِ إِلَّا أَن تَكُونَ تِجَارَةً عَن تَرَاضٍ مِّنكُمْ﴾$$

"O you who have believed, do not consume one another's wealth unjustly but only [in lawful] business by mutual consent" [TMQ An-Nisa': 29]

He said:

التجارةُ رزقٌ من رزقِ الله، وحلالٌ من حلالِ الله لمن طَلَبها بصدقِها وبِرّها، وقد كنا نُحَدَّثُ أن التاجرَ الأمينَ الصدوق مع السبعة في ظل العرش يوم القيامة

"The Tijaarah (trade) is sustenance from the sustenance of Allah. It is a Halal from the Halal of Allah for the one who seeks it honestly and righteously. We used to relate that the honest trustworthy trader is among the seven in the shade of Allah on the Day of Judgement" [107].

Here, in this piece of guidance, he brought together the texts related to the condemnation of the traders, like his statement ﷺ:

$$إِنَّ التُّجَّارَ هُمُ الفُجَّار$$

"Verily, the traders are corrupted immoral people (*Fujjar*)".

They asked: "O Messenger of Allah, did Allah not make trade Halal and prohibited usury? He said:

$$بَلَى وَلَكِنَّهُمْ يَحْلِفُونَ وَيَأْثَمُونَ$$

---

[107] Tafsir At-Tabari (6/630).

"Indeed, (that is true) however, they swear oaths and act sinfully"
[108]

And the texts of commendation and praise like His *Qawl* تعالى:

$$﴿فَإِذَا قُضِيَتِ الصَّلَاةُ فَانتَشِرُوا فِي الْأَرْضِ وَابْتَغُوا مِن فَضْلِ اللَّهِ وَاذْكُرُوا اللَّهَ كَثِيرًا لَّعَلَّكُمْ تُفْلِحُونَ﴾$$

"And when the prayer has been concluded, disperse within the land and seek from the bounty of Allah, and remember Allah often that you may be successful"   [TMQ Al-Jumu'ah: 10]

And the *Fadl* (bounty) of Allah here means trade [109]

'Umar, may Allah be pleased with him, said:

ما جاءني أجلي في مكان ما عدا في سبيل الله عز وجل أحبُّ إلي من أن يأتيني وأنا بين شعبتي رحلي أطلب من فضل الله

"There is no place in which my time (i.e. of death) will come to me, asides from in the way of Allah, that is more beloved to me than that if it comes to me whilst I am with my saddlebag seeking the Fadl (bounty) of Allah".

He then recited:

$$﴿وَآخَرُونَ يَضْرِبُونَ فِي الْأَرْضِ يَبْتَغُونَ مِن فَضْلِ اللَّهِ﴾$$

"And others travel through the land seeking from the bounty of Allah"

---

[108] Al-Imam Ahmad, Musnad Al-Makiyeen, Hadith Abdur Rahman bin Shibl, Hadith number: (2/15666). Shu'aib Al-Arna'ut said: [Its Isnad is Sahih.

[109] Refer to: Tafsir Ash-Shinqity (6/77).

[TMQ Al-Muzzammil: 20][110].

He, may Allah be pleased with him, extracted this point of guidance from the context of the verse as the Ayah continues stating:

$$﴿وَآخَرُونَ يُقَاتِلُونَ فِي سَبِيلِ اللَّهِ﴾$$

"And others fighting in the way of Allah"　　　　[TMQ Al-Muzzammil: 20]

This is as combining and reconciling between two evidences is more appropriate than working in accordance with one of them only, as stated by the principle of the scholars of Usool.

He ﷺ said in a Hadith related by 'Amr bin Al-'Aas, may Allah be pleased with him:

$$نِعْمَ الْمَالُ الصَّالِحُ لِلْمَرْءِ الصَّالِحِ$$

"Excellent is the honest property for the righteous person" [111]

There is also the Hadith related by Abu Sa'eed Al-Khudri, may Allah be pleased with him:

$$التَّاجِرُ الصَّدُوقُ الأَمِينُ مَعَ النَّبِيِّينَ وَالصِّدِّيقِينَ وَالشُّهَدَاءِ$$

"The truthful (honest), trustworthy trader is with the Prophets, the truthful, and the martyrs" [112]

---

[110] Shu'ab Al-*Iman*, Al-Baihaqi, At-*Tawakkul* Billah (2/450).

[111] Al-Bukhari, *Al-Adab* Al-Mufrad, chapter: The honest property for the righteous man, Hadith number: (299). Al-Albani classified it as Sahih in his "Sahih *Al-Adab* Al-Mufrad" (p 126).

[112] At-Tirmidhi, Chapters of sales, chapter: What came related to the traders, Hadith number: (1209). He said: [This Hadith is Hasan]. Al-Albani classified it as Da'eef (weak) in his "Da'eef Sunan At-Tirmidhi" (P 145).

Ibn ul-'Arabiy (DoD: 543 AH), may Allah's mercy be upon him, said:

هذا الحديث وإن، لم يبلغ درجة المتفق عليه من الصحيح فإن معناه صحيح؛ لأنه جمع الصدق والشهادة بالحق والنصح للخلق وامتثال الأمر المتوجه إليه من قبل الرسول

"Even if this Hadith does not reach the grade of being agreed upon from the Sahih (Hadith), its meaning is correct. That is because it combined truthfulness (honesty) and martyrdom with the *Haqq* (truth), sincerity towards the creation and compliance to the command that the Messenger ﷺ directed to him" [113]

The greatest means for attaining property is the profitable trade and most of the means of sustenance are connected to it [114]. This highlights the depth of understanding in the reported tradition (Athar). That is because it encourages trade to be undertaken upon the basis of honesty and righteousness. The one who reflects upon all the economic issues finds that they return to two great fundamentals: The acquisition of Halal property and spending it in permissible areas of spending [115].

The noble Taabi'iy Qatadah (DoD: 117 AH) delved deeply into the meanings of the verse, making clear to the people the virtues of the *Deen* and *Dunyaa* when the trade is undertaken in accordance with its Shar'iy (legal) condition. That is found in his statement: [**For the one who seeks it honestly and righteously**]. As such, Al-Imam At-Tabari (DoD: 310 AH) benefited from him in his Tafsir and consequently said at this verse: [In this verse there is a clarification

---

[113] 'Aridat ul-Ahwadhi, Ibn ul-'Arabi: (5/168).
[114] Refer to: Tafsir Az-Zamakhshari (1/502).
[115] Refer to: Tafsir Ash-Shinqiti (6/77).

from Allah ﺗﻌﺎﻟﯽ repudiating the view of the ignorant from the Sufis who deny seeking the sources of sustenance from acts of trade and manufacturing (or craftmanship)] [116].

Observing concepts such as these in trade and economics means the revival of the values of honesty and righteousness within the society, as it represents an economic beacon of light and moral illumination. This is from the great effects of the *Tadabbur* (deep thought and contemplation) upon the Qur'an Al-Karim. That is as it reflects a source of revival for the Ummah in all areas of life, including the economic aspect through which the affairs of the people among themselves are made good and upright and are governed by elevated moral principles.

O honourable traders! Holding fast to the teachings of the *Sharee'ah* in all aspects of life is a blessing upon the person and the society. And contemplate how the Islamic concept of trading and material acquisition was transformed into abundant reward in the hereafter which reaches to making you, by Allah's permission, under the shade of Allah on the day that there is no shade except His, on the condition of honesty and righteousness. So glad tidings are due to the trustworthy and honest trader!

---

[116] Tafsir At-Tabari (6/629).

Discharging Mercy and Good Treatment

The family is a primary focus of Islam and subject of concern and care in the *Sharee'ah*. That is because it represents the primary institution of the society, the factory for producing men, the cradle for generations and the nucleus of the society.

Islam's care towards the family was apparent from its inception. That was demonstrated by the invitation to make the best choice in respect to selecting a companion and partner. He ﷺ said addressing men:

فَاظْفَرْ بِذَاتِ الدِّينِ تَرِبَتْ يَدَاكَ

"Select the one possessing the *Deen* and you will prosper" [117].

And he ﷺ said to the woman and her guardians:

إِذَا جَاءَكُمْ مَنْ تَرْضَوْنَ دِينَهُ وَخُلُقَهُ فَأَنْكِحُوهُ إِلاَّ تَفْعَلُوا تَكُنْ فِتْنَةٌ فِي الأَرْضِ وَفَسَادٌ عَرِيضٌ

"When someone whose *Deen* and character are pleasing to you comes to you, then marry him. If you do not do so, then there will be turmoil (Fitnah) in the land and wide corruption (Fasad)" [118]

---

[117] Al-Bukhari, book of Nikah (marriage), chapter: Al-Akifaa' Fee d-*Deen*, Hadith number (5090). Muslim, book of Ar-Ridaa' (wet-nursing), chapter: Recommendation of marrying the one possessing the *Deen*, Hadith number (1466), related by Abu Hurairah.

[118] At-Tirmidhi, Chapters of marriage, chapter: Whoever comes to you whose *Deen* pleases you, Hadith number (1085), related by Hatim Al-Muzani. He said: [This Hadith is Hasan Ghareeb] and Al-Albani classified it as Hasan Li-Ghairihi. Refer to: Irwaa' ul-Ghaleel (6/268).

This care reaches those great legislations which determine the rulings related to the end of the marital life. Consequently, we find utmost justice within the rulings of divorce in Islam.

And we find completeness in the rulings related to the waiting period and mourning, in a clear exaltation of that firm contract (of marriage):

﴿وَأَخَذْنَ مِنكُم مِّيثَاقًا غَلِيظًا﴾

"And they have taken from you a firm and strong covenant"

[TMQ An-Nisa': 21]

As marriage is a firm and strong covenant, Allah تعالى has assumed by Himself the organization of this institution by making clear the obligations and rights for the two pillars of the family and its main supporting blocks: The husband and wife. This has been done by organisation, precision, justice and safeguarding the family from the disturbances caused by desires and the winds of disagreements, and to avert the factors that lead to demolition and destruction.

From the beauties of the insightful readings of the *Salaf* (predecessors) of these legislative meanings from the Book of Allah, is what Al-Imam At-Tabari (DoD: 310 AH) attributed to Ibn 'Abbas, may Allah be pleased with them both, concerning His statement: تعالى

﴿الرِّجَالُ قَوَّامُونَ عَلَى النِّسَاءِ﴾

"Men are the guardians (protectors and maintainers) of women"

[TMQ An-Nisa': 34]

He, may Allah be pleased with him, said:

أمراء! عليها أن تُطِيعَه فيما أمَرها اللهُ به من طاعتِهِ، وطاعتُه: أن تكونَ مُحْسِنةً
إلى أهلِهِ، حافِظَةً لمالِه، وفضلُه عليها بنفَقتِه وسَعْيِه

"It means Umaraa' (Leaders /commanders)! She must obey him in that which Allah has commanded her with in terms of obedience. Obedience to him means: That she is good to his family and safeguards his property whilst his favour upon her is manifested in his Nafaqah (spending) and efforts (i.e. work)" [119].

Here, he, may Allah be pleased with him, has explained the rights of every party with concise words and eloquent explanation. If you thought deeply in this narration, in light of the *Sharee'ah* of Allah in contrast to the laws of man, you would perceive wisdom, justice, and true nature. Through that, the artificial clash between the two sexes would vanish. Instead, the slogan or banner of this partnership would come to be: Affection and mercy, love and blessing:

﴿وَمِنْ آيَاتِهِ أَنْ خَلَقَ لَكُم مِّنْ أَنفُسِكُمْ أَزْوَاجًا لِّتَسْكُنُوا إِلَيْهَا وَجَعَلَ بَيْنَكُم مَّوَدَّةً وَرَحْمَةً ۚ إِنَّ فِي ذَٰلِكَ لَآيَاتٍ لِّقَوْمٍ يَتَفَكَّرُونَ﴾

"And among His Signs is that He created for you wives from among yourselves, that you may find repose (or comfort) in them, and He has put between you affection and mercy. Verily, in that are indeed signs for a people who reflect"   [TMQ Ar-Rum: 21]

From that which distinguishes the Islamic legislation (from other legislations) is how it links the rights to the obligations:

---

[119] Tafsir At-Tabari (6/687).

$$﴿وَلَهُنَّ مِثْلُ الَّذِي عَلَيْهِنَّ بِالْمَعْرُوفِ﴾$$

"And they (women) have rights similar (to those of their husbands) over them (as regards obedience and respect, etc.) in accordance with what is reasonable (or fair)"   [TMQ Al-Baqarah: 228]

This reflects the greatest level of completion in respect to building individual responsibility and preparing the marital pair to enter this great partnership.

The preparation of the woman for the institution of marriage includes teaching her what she has due to her and what is due upon her, in relation to explaining her rights and obligations. That produces stability for the woman and the family as a result. This narration before us clarifies the principles related to the woman's obligations in Islam and we also find within it how the uprightness of the woman extends to reach the family of her husband and his property. **It may be that this narration (of Ibn 'Abbas) is from the clearest and most explicit of narrations in respect to encouraging the wife to treat the family of her husband well and to deal with them with goodness and excellent treatment.**

Prophetic Ahadeeth have come explaining these obligations also focusing upon these meanings. That is like the Hadith related by Abu Hurairah from the Prophet ﷺ:

$$خَيْرُ نِسَاء رَكِبْنَ الْإِبِل صَالِح نِسَاء قُرَيْش أَحْنَاهُ عَلَى وَلَدٍ فِي صِغَرِهِ وَأَرْعَاهُ عَلَى زَوْجٍ$$

$$فِي ذَاتِ يَدِهِ$$

The best of the women who have ridden on camels are the upright women of Quraish, for they are the most affectionate to children when they are young **and the most observant and caring over what belongs to their husbands** [120].

Al-Hafizh Al-'Iraqi (DoD: 806 AH) said:

"Its intended meaning is her safeguarding of her husband's property (wealth) and the good management of it in terms of spending and other than that, in addition to safeguarding it from the causes of damage" [121].

It is therefore understood from this obligation that the protection and maintenance (*Qiwamah*) of the man over the wife represents sufficing the woman. This sufficiency does not however mean squandering but rather the caretaking of the wealth (or property) of the husband just as he, may Allah be pleased with him, said in the narration: "She safeguards his property (or wealth)".

The fragrance of the uprightness of the woman reaches the family of her husband. This foundational principle is not just a theory but rather is established by the biographies of the righteous women, at the forefront of whom is the beloved of the Messenger of Allah ﷺ, the Mother of Believers 'Aa'ishah, may Allah be pleased with her. In a Hadith related by 'Urwah bin Az-Zubair, may Allah's mercy be upon him, concerning 'Aa'ishah, may Allah be pleased with her, he said:

وَكَانَتْ أَرَقَّ شَىْءٍ لِقَرَابَتِهِمْ مِنْ رَسُولِ اللَّهِ ﷺ

---

[120] Al-Bukhari, book of Nafaqat (spending), chapter: The woman's safeguarding of that belonging to him, Hadith number (5365). Muslim, book of Fada'il (virtues), chapter: From the virtues of the women of Quraish, Hadith number (2527).

[121] Tarh At-Tathreeb (7/14).

"She used to treat them (the people of Bani Zuhrah) well due to their relation to the Messenger of Allah ﷺ"[122].

A nice point here is that the relater is from her main relations, the son of her sister and foster son 'Urwah bin Az-Zubair. Further to that, it is amazing that this took place after the passing of the Messenger of Allah ﷺ, so, how great was the goodness of the covenant and faithfulness to it!

Ibn ul-Qayyim (DoD: 751), may Allah's mercy be upon him, said when presenting his affirmation of the wife's service to her husband, which is from the issues based upon the guardianship (Qiwamah) of the man: [Here is the noblest of the women of the worlds (meaning Fatimah Az-Zahrah, may Allah be pleased with her). She used to serve her husband and she came to him complaining to him about the service but he did not remove the cause of her complaint] [123]

The woman submitting to the command of the husband and his guardianship (Qiwamah) over her is from her completion, *Taqwaa* (piety) and self-honour. The submission of the woman to this divine command does not therefore reflect a weakness in her or a reduction of her worth or value.

From the amazing radiances (*Mashaariq*) of the verse:

$$﴿الرِّجَالُ قَوَّامُونَ عَلَى النِّسَاءِ﴾$$

"Men are the guardians (protectors and maintainers) of women"

---

[122] Al-Bukhari, the Book of Al-Manaqib, chapter: Manaqib Quraish, Hadith number (3503).
[123] Zaad ul-Ma'aad (5/171).

Is what Ibn 'Aashour (DoD: 1393 AH) said:

وقيام الرجال على النساء هو قيام الحفظ والدفاع، وقيام الاكتساب والإنتاج المالي

"Men being guardians over women means undertaking the maintenance and protection and to undertake material acquisition and financial production" [124]

O honourable women! Concerning the verse:

﴿الرِّجَالُ قَوَّامُونَ عَلَى النِّسَاءِ﴾

"Men are the protectors and maintainers of women"   [TMQ An-Nisa': 34]

It is legislation for the sake of the woman, for her interest and protection. It is not to oppress and humiliate her. It is sufficient in this regard that the affirmation of the right of guardianship for the man came in the Surah, which revolves around the affirmation of the rights of the women. It dictates that she be spent upon, that he makes efforts for that, and that she be maintained and defended! This guardianship, which is apparently related to the right of the man, is interpreted to reflect the rights of the woman, where the guardianship over her means maintenance, defence, mercy and good treatment. That is from the secrets of the *Sharee'ah* of Al-Lateef Al-Khabeer (The Kind, the All-Aware).

---

[124] Tafsir Ibn 'Aashour (5/38).

To Every Reformer

Reform is the greatest objective of the revealed messages and the highest aim of the Qur'an. This is evident in some of the verses and alluded to in others:

﴿وَلَا تُفْسِدُوا فِي الْأَرْضِ بَعْدَ إِصْلَاحِهَا وَادْعُوهُ خَوْفًا وَطَمَعًا ۚ إِنَّ رَحْمَتَ اللَّهِ قَرِيبٌ مِّنَ الْمُحْسِنِينَ﴾

"And cause not corruption upon the earth after its reformation. And invoke Him in fear and aspiration. Indeed, the mercy of Allah is near to the doers of good" [TMQ Al-A'araf: 56]

This represents the cause of the salvation of nations and the continuation of states and civilizations. It was expressed explicitly in the speech of Allah تعالى:

﴿وَمَا كَانَ رَبُّكَ لِيُهْلِكَ الْقُرَىٰ بِظُلْمٍ وَأَهْلُهَا مُصْلِحُونَ﴾

"And your Lord would not have destroyed the cities unjustly while their people were engaged in reformation" [TMQ Hud: 117]

This is a text that is not open to interpretation. It is evident and not outweighed, literal (*Haqiqah*) and not metaphorical (*Majaz*).

The pivotal cause is reformation (*Islaah*) and not just uprightness (*Salaah*). The person whom the Qur'an desires is the *Muslih* (reformer) and not the secluded upright or righteous person (*Saalih*). Life is radiated by reformers and is made happy by them, those who are the pioneers of the Ummah and its vanguard.

As the path of reform is surrounded by difficulties and discomforts, the one who seeks reform is assisted by Allah تعالى. That is as Ibn 'Abbas, may Allah be pleased with them both, explained concerning the His statement تعالى:

﴿إِن يُرِيدَا إِصْلَاحًا يُوَفِّقِ اللَّهُ بَيْنَهُمَا﴾

"If they both desire rectification (Islaah), Allah will cause their reconciliation"   [TMQ An-Nisa': 35]

He said:

وذلك الحكمان، وكذلك كلُّ مُصْلِحٍ يُوَفِّقُه اللهُ للحق والصواب

"That is for the two arbitrators and similarly it applies in respect to every *Muslih* (reformer). Allah grants him *Tawfiq* (reconciliation) towards the truth and what is correct" [125]

The *Tawfiq* (reconciliation) is a divine gift which people strive for, so that affection and love prevail in the homes, peace and security pervade in the society and in order to provide life with meaning and delight. It is the water of life and its beating heart as what is life if the person is deprived of the *Tawfiq* of His *Rabb* (lord).

This divine promise contains a motivation for reformation within the Muslim society. That is because it is from the greatest incentives for the self to bear the perils of reform and what it entails in terms of effort, sacrifices, and risk. So, all difficult matters are made easy when they settle in the inner self of the believer:

---

[125] Tafsir At-Tabari (6/730).

كلُّ مُصْلِحٍ يُوَفِّقُه اللهُ للحق والصواب

"Allah grants every *Muslih* (reformer) *Tawfiq* (reconciliation and help) towards the truth and what is correct"

This dissemination provides an education from him, may Allah be pleased with him, for those reading the paths of contemplation (*Tadabbur*) and its paths through which the exhortations of the Qur'an and its distinguishing radiances are extracted. That is through the beautiful deduction from the verse that every reformer, if sincere in intention, is granted *Tawfiq* from Allah towards the truth and what is correct.

One of the greatest points of this narrated tradition (of Ibn 'Abbas) is that it contains within it guidance for the reformation of the reformers by drawing their attention to the importance of the intention and the basis of the *Tawfiq*, which is the **"Salaah (wellbeing and uprightness) of the heart"**. That is as the heart informs the reformers of the secret of success along their path and of the causes of failure.

Al-Imam Ibn Taymiyah (DoD: 728 AH), may Allah's mercy be upon him, said: "Allah سبحانه has tied the *Islaah* (reform), which He provides reward for, to "*Al-Ikhlaas*" (sincerity). That is as He said:

﴿وَمَن يَفْعَلْ ذَٰلِكَ ابْتِغَاءَ مَرْضَاتِ اللَّهِ فَسَوْفَ نُؤْتِيهِ أَجْرًا عَظِيمًا﴾

"*And he who does this, seeking the good Pleasure of Allah, We shall give him a great reward*" [TMQ An-Nisa': 114]

Many of the people engage in *Islaah* either for fame (reputation) or to show off" [126]

He, may Allah be pleased with him, deduced from the information of the verse that the one who makes right his intention in a matter that he is seeking to accomplish, then Allah will make right his aspiration whilst calamity or misfortune is linked to the corruption of the intention [127]. Consequently, it is the reformers who are the pioneers whilst those who most need to be reformed are the pioneers. How can the shadow be upright and straight if the stick is crooked?!

Reform is not merely a claim as there is a difference between reform and its claim. The dissemination of Ibn 'Abbas, may Allah be pleased with him, is supported by the disseminations of the *Sharee'ah* in the subject area of reform in general. Just as the *Tawfiq* granted to every *Muslih* (reformer) in every field from among the fields of goodness and giving is supported by the disseminations of the *Sharee'ah*.

So how happy are the truthful reformers and how great is their reward!

---

[126] Majmoo' Fataawaa Ash-Sheikh ul-Islam Ibn Taymiyah (11/550).

[127] Refer to: Tafsir Ar-Raaghib (3/1228).

The Measure of Actions

In the moments of demise at the time of the final farewell accompanied by the fright of the moment and the pain of the agony of death, there is no place for pretence or acting. At that time, the concealed matters of the inner selves and the truths of the hearts manifest. The *'Ulamaa* (scholars), may Allah have mercy upon them, said:

قد أجرى الكريم عادته بكرمه أنه من عاش على شيء مات عليه، ومن مات على شيء بُعِث عليه

"Al-Karim (Allah تعالى) sets His custom into motion by His Karam (magnanimity). That the one who lives upon something dies upon it and whoever dies upon something is resurrected upon it"[128]

It was in such moments that they visited 'Amir bin Abdullah Al-'Anbari (DoD: prior to 60 AH) and found him crying. They asked him: "What has caused you to cry, whilst you had been such and such, and such and such?" He replied: "I am crying because I hear Allah saying:

﴿إِنَّمَا يَتَقَبَّلُ اللَّهُ مِنَ الْمُتَّقِينَ﴾

"Verily, Allah accepts only from those who are Al-Muttaqeen (pious and God-fearing)" [TMQ Al-Ma'idah: 27] [129]

The best conclusion for a person in this life is that it is concluded for him through the contemplation of the Qur'an accompanied by knowledge of the true reality of piety (*Taqwaa*) and reform (*Islaah*).

---

[128] Tafsir Ibn Kathir (2/87).
[129] Tafsir At-Tabari (8/327-328).

Contemplation of the Qur'an at that moment awakens the heart to emulate positions like theirs, may Allah have mercy upon them, and to pay dear attention to attaining the conditions of the acceptance of the righteous action whilst fearing conceit and that which makes the actions amount to nothing.

We observe in this difficult moment an important feature from among the features of reforming the self by way of *Tadabbur* (contemplation) as undertaken by the *Salaf* (righteous predecessors). That is by making it extend in length to reach the extent of the whole life's duration. It is the reforming of the self that does not come to an end until the moment of death, just like in this reported tradition (*Athar*). It is a continuous and non-ending reformation that makes the contemplator not slacken from reforming himself and rectifying it throughout his life. The contemplation has removed from him the cloak of conceit and smugness and made him aware of his own faults. He then continues to strive with himself upon the path of reforming his *Nafs* (self) until Allah تعالى brings about his death.

As for the secret of these tears, then we do not find a clear and eloquent statement as great as that of Abu Ad-Darda', may Allah be pleased with him:

لأن أستيقن أن الله قد تقبل مني صلاةً واحدةً أحب إليّ من الدنيا وما فيها، إن

الله يقول

"That I ascertain that Allah has accepted from me one single prayer is more beloved to me than the *Dunyaa* (worldly life) and all that is in it. Verily, Allah says:

﴿قَالَ إِنَّمَا يَتَقَبَّلُ اللَّهُ مِنَ الْمُتَّقِينَ﴾

"He said: Verily, Allah accepts only from those who are Al-Muttaqeen (pious)" [TMQ Al-Ma'idah: 27] [130]

The true measure for actions is, therefore, their being accepted by Allah تعالى, and it is through them that abundance is accomplished.

This understanding, if understood by implication from this story, has come in an explicit manner in the reported tradition which At-Tabari (DoD: 310 AH) attributed to Qatadah (DoD: 117 AH), may Allah's mercy be upon him, concerning His *Qawl* (statement) تعالى:

﴿وَلَا يَذْكُرُونَ اللَّهَ إِلَّا قَلِيلًا﴾

"And they do not remember Allah except a little" [TMQ An-Nisa': 142]

He said:

إنما قَلَّ ذِكْرُ المنافق؛ لأن الله لم يقبله، وكلُّ ما ردَّ اللَّهُ قليل، وكل ما قَبِل الله كثير

"The remembrance of the hypocrite was little as Allah did not accept it and all that Allah rejects is little while all that Allah accepts is much" [131]

Was it not Allah who stated when recalling the speech of Al-Khalil (Ibrahim), peace be upon him:

﴿رَبَّنَا تَقَبَّلْ مِنَّا ۖ إِنَّكَ أَنتَ السَّمِيعُ الْعَلِيمُ﴾

"Our Lord! Accept (this service) from us. Verily! You are the All-Hearer, the All-Knower" [TMQ Al-Baqarah: 127]

---

[130] Tafsir Ibn Kathir (3/85), transmitted from Ibn Abi Hatim

[131] Tafsir At-Tabari (7/614).

Wuhaib bin Al-Ward (DoD: 135 AH) said:

يا خليل الرحمن! ترفع قوائم بيت الرحمن، وأنت مشفق أن لا يتقبل منك

"O Khalil Ar-Rahman! You are raising the pillars of the House of Ar-Rahman and (yet) you are (still) concerned that it may not be accepted from you!" [132]

The pivotal issue is not the quantity, in terms of how much you have prayed or how much you have given in *Sadaqah*, it relates to how and whether you have met the conditions of acceptance? There is a major difference between the one who is concerned about the action and the one who is concerned about the acceptance of the action. This difference is comprehended by the one who has reached the levels of comprehension and whose *Iman* has blended with the happiness of the heart.

This represents the fundamental measure for the actions, whether large or small. Its measure is the acceptance of Allah, and in accordance with that, the abundance and littleness (or insignificance) is measured.

This contemplation makes the believer pay attention to the spirit of the action, and that is sincerity. He pays attention to his intention and examines his heart in the action. The *Shaytan* (devil) only comes to the person when these effects are absent from him. It is when they pay attention to the form of the action and neglect the spirit of the action. How great our need is to be reminded of this in an age where people have come to act in the absence of appreciation. Within this reported tradition there is an aspect of what they aspire to. That is because they desire the sweetness of

---

[132] Tafsir Ibn Kathir (1/427).

the action and as such, they seek to perfect the inner elements and pay attention to the secret matters.

The quoted tradition also contains a reminder to remove conceit from the inner self as that is one of the most significant destructive flaws. It also contains an indication to the diligence of the *Salaf* (righteous predecessors) in respect to warning the people away from treading the path of the hypocrites in relation to remembering Allah a little. That is in addition to their great care and attention provided to extolling the actions which Allah تعالى accepts and diligence upon attaining that acceptance.

O contented one, happiness in life which you aspire for does not lie except in observing this important measure, and that is: "The concern for sincerity and acceptance". Concerning this Al-Imam Ibn Taymiyah (DoD: 728 AH), may Allah's mercy be upon him, said: [The happy (or contented) one fears in his actions that he is not truthful in his sincerity to Allah in the *Deen* or that they (the actions) will not be in conformity to what Allah commanded upon the tongue of His Messenger. For this reason, the *Salaf* use to fear hypocrisy in respect to themselves. Al-Bukhari mentioned from Abu Al-'Aaliyah who said: "I met thirty of the companions of Muhammad ﷺ and each one of them feared hypocrisy in respect to himself. As such, they used to make exceptions where one of them would say: "I am a believer if Allah wills". Those like them would seek the forgiveness of Allah for what they knew about and what they did not know about in terms of shortcomings and transgression and repent for that" [133]

---

[133] Jaami' Ar-Rasaa'il, Ibn Taymiyah (1/257).

Discontent with the Actions of the Truthful

Allah opened the canopy of the Qur'an with a discussion concerning the different categories of people. The greatest share of the discussion of Al-Baqarah in its amazing early part is concerning the third category, the last in discussion but the first in respect to warning and caution.

The discussion concerning the hypocrites extends throughout the Qur'an. At the end of the ten long Surahs, the discussion in Surah At-Tawbah revolves around them. The great scholar of the Ummah Ibn 'Abbas, may Allah be pleased with him, said:

التوبة هي الفاضحة، ما زالت تنزل، ومنهم ومنهم، حتى ظنوا أنها لن تبقي أحدًا منهم إلا ذكر فيها

"At-Tawbah is the exposer, it continued to be revealed stating "and from them", "and from them", until they believed that nobody would be left remaining from among them except that he would be mentioned in it"[134].

Then in the Mufassal (category of Surahs), which is the Muhkam of the Qur'an, we find a whole Surah that has been given the name of "Al-Munafiqun" (The Hypocrites).

This detailed discussion of the hypocrites makes the contemplator of the Book of Allah aware of the past of the hypocrites and capable of looking out for their future. Such insight does not come to other than the contemplator of the Qur'an Al-'Azheem.

---

[134] Al-Bukhari, Book of Tafsir Al-Qur'an, Hadith number (4882).

Al-Imam At-Tabari (DoD: 310 AH) attributed to Al-Hasan Al-Basri (DoD: 110 AH), may Allah's mercy be upon him, concerning the statement of Allah تعالى:

﴿يَا أَيُّهَا الَّذِينَ آمَنُوا عَلَيْكُمْ أَنفُسَكُمْ ۖ لَا يَضُرُّكُم مَّن ضَلَّ إِذَا اهْتَدَيْتُمْ﴾

"O you who have believed, upon you is [responsibility for] yourselves. Those who have gone astray will not harm you when you have been guided" [TMQ Al-Ma'idah: 105]

الحمدُ للهِ بِها، والحمدُ للهِ عليها، ما كان مؤمنٌ فيما مضى، ولا مؤمنٌ فيما بَقِي، إلا

وإلى جانبه منافقٌ يكرَهُ عملَه

He said: "All praise (Al-Hamd) belongs to Allah through it and All praise belongs to Allah upon it. There was no believer in the past and no believer who remains (i.e. in the present or future), except that he has a Munaafiq (hypocrite) by his side who hates his action" [135]

Therefore, from the history, he, may Allah's mercy be upon him, proceeded to look forward to their future. This reflects deep contemplation and understanding of the people. That is because history repeats itself, and people are people. So, just as those who transgress and oppress have companions in the past, the hypocrites also have a connection to the past, and as such, the believers are not over-concerned by the newly occurring names and titles.

This contemplation came blended with an explorative reading of the Qur'an and contemplation concerning the reality of the people. We can see, in his contemplation, insight into the future of

---

[135] Tafsir At-Tabari (9/50).

the people. However, the impactful factor in his contemplation was his deduction, may Allah's mercy be upon him, that the dislike for the righteous action is hypocrisy. The scholars of Tafsir understood that by "The action of the believer" Al Hasan meant the commanding of the *Ma'roof* (good) and forbidding of the *Munkar* (evil) [136]. However, his statement most likely indicates to the generality of the action of the believer, whilst the most prominent of the actions of the believer, in which their dislike or hatred manifests, is the commanding of the *Ma'roof* and the forbidding of the *Munkar*.

This meaning has supporting evidence. In Surah At-Tawbah we find the hypocrites defaming the truthful in a blatant manner:

﴿الَّذِينَ يَلْمِزُونَ الْمُطَّوِّعِينَ مِنَ الْمُؤْمِنِينَ فِي الصَّدَقَاتِ وَالَّذِينَ لَا يَجِدُونَ إِلَّا جُهْدَهُمْ فَيَسْخَرُونَ مِنْهُمْ ۙ سَخِرَ اللَّهُ مِنْهُمْ وَلَهُمْ عَذَابٌ أَلِيمٌ﴾

"Those who defame the believers who give charity (in Allah's Cause) voluntarily, and those who could not find to give charity (in Allah's Cause) except what is available to them. So they mock at them (believers). Allah will throw back their mockery upon them, and they shall have a painful punishment" [TMQ At-Taubah: 79]

Mockery is a sign of hatred. It is enough for the person in terms of abandonment of Allah to hate the righteous action, let alone undertake it. This is the way of the hypocrites and disbelievers throughout the ages. Such hatred evolves with the evolution of time. In our current time, we find the people of desires employing technological development to mock the actions of the truthful and righteous and making use of the media to spread their hateful

---

136 Refer to: Tafsir At-Tabari (9/50, Tafsir Ath-Tha'labi (4/115) and Tafsir Ibn Kathir (3/215).

speech and broadcast their specious arguments to generate doubts.

The purpose behind familiarising the believers with the attributes of hypocrisy is to strengthen them and make them firm. That is so that they don't weaken in *Iman* and the mockery of the hypocrites does not dissuade them from the righteous action. Rather, they continue upon their path and anticipate the suffering that accompanies the righteous act.

Indeed, Al-Baqaa'iy (DoD: 885 AH) transmitted from Al-Haraaliy (DoD: 638 AH) significant radiances concerning the meaning of the tradition of Al-Hasan Al-Basri (DoD: 110 AH). He said:

"The hypocrite looks at what he can use to bring down the virtues of the people of virtue and turns a blind eye to their good qualities. It is like what has been related in that Allah hates the one who leaves the good of the believer and takes his bad. The truthful believer disregards the faults of the people of faults, so what is the situation with the one who seeks the flaws of the people of good characteristics!

ومِن أظهر علامات المنافق تبرُّمُه بأعمال الصادق

From the most blatant (or prominent) signs of the hypocrite is his discontent with the actions of the righteous][137]

The danger of hidden hypocrisy lies in it being a warning for the disease of the heart. If the person is not alert to that, the disease will develop, and apparent hypocrisy will become dreadful, may refuge be sought in Allah from that. It represents the first step of *Shaytan* (the devil) if the person does not employ effort to repel it,

---

[137] Nazham Ad-Durar (8/538).

as it leads to what is worse. The well-being of the heart is most entitled to care, and the person who strives with his inner self and purifies his heart has succeeded and is filled with joy by the actions of the truthful and the achievements of the righteous.

From the Characteristics of the Great Personalities

From the great decorations of honour in the life of this world is affiliation to the school of the great Prophets and for the thinking to plunge into the perfections of those souls whom Allah تعالى wanted to be lamps of guidance and radiances of light for humanity.

That school did not know walled dormitories or imposing fences. That is because its lessons were signs for those who question:

﴿لَّقَدْ كَانَ فِي يُوسُفَ وَإِخْوَتِهِ آيَاتٌ لِّلسَّائِلِينَ﴾

"Verily, in Yusuf and his brethren, there were signs for those who question" [TMQ Yusuf: 7]

Its degrees were guidance for those following the path and its certifications were a mercy for the worlds.

That school is ancient in the caverns of history. It is the oldest school known to mankind, beginning with Adam, peace be upon him, with its maturing fruits extending across generations until Allah inherits the earth and all who are upon it. It is from the greatest of what benefits the people:

﴿وَأَمَّا مَا يَنفَعُ النَّاسَ فَيَمْكُثُ فِي الْأَرْضِ﴾

"But as for that which benefits the people, then it remains on the earth" [TMQ Ar-Ra'd: 17]

The major foundations of that heavenly university and divine school include:

The teaching of "*Akhlaq*" (moral characteristics). That is as the good *Akhlaq* represents an ancient fundamental basis within the

Prophetic laws which has been untouched by abrogation and has not been subjected to restriction or exception.

You will find pages radiating with the good characteristics and brilliant illuminations related to refining the inner selves. That is because the *Akhlaq* were not a voluntary choice within the Prophetic school but were rather a part of the essence of the Aqeedah (belief), blended with it to the point that the *Deen* itself has been called "*Khuluq*" (moral character). Allah تعالى said:

$$﴿إِنَّكَ لَعَلَىٰ خُلُقٍ عَظِيمٍ﴾$$

"Indeed, you are upon a great moral character (Khuluq)"

[TMQ Al-Qalam: 4]

Ibn 'Abbas, may Allah be pleased with them both, said in his interpretation of this verse:

إنك على دين عظيم، وهو الإسلام

"Verily, you are upon a great *Deen* and it is Islam" [138]

Naming a matter by a part of it is evidence for the greatness of this part, its being pivotal and that it is a pillar from among the pillars of that matter [139].

There is no place that the Qur'an presents to us the effusions of this school except that it brings forth through them a great lesson related to *Akhlaq*, conduct, and dealing with others.

In relation to the terrifying situation of the Day of Judgement, the Qur'an informs us of the great *Akhlaq* of the Prophets. Despite the

---

[138] Tafsir At-Tabari (23/150).
[139] Refer to: Tafsir Ibn 'Atiyah (1/434), Tafsir Al-Baidawiy (2/16) and Tafsir Ibn Juzaiy (1/152).

terror of the situation and graveness of the matter, the *Akhlaq* of the Prophets radiate like the sun. These *Akhlaq* were the subject of the contemplation of the *Salaf* (righteous predecessors) and the subject of their deduction. Al-Imam At-Tabari (DoD: 310 AH) attributed to Qatadah (DoD: 117), may Allah's mercy be upon him, concerning His statement تعالى:

﴿إِن تُعَذِّبْهُمْ فَإِنَّهُمْ عِبَادُكَ ۖ وَإِن تَغْفِرْ لَهُمْ فَإِنَّكَ أَنتَ الْعَزِيزُ الْحَكِيمُ﴾

"If You should punish them, (then) indeed they are Your servants; but if You forgive them, (then) indeed it is You who is the Exalted in Might, the Wise" [TMQ Al-Ma'idah: 118]

He said:

والله ما كانوا [أي: الرسل] طعَّانين ولا لعَّانين!

"By Allah, they (i.e. the Messengers) were not those who defamed and cursed (others)"[140].

Here, you will be filled with wonder and covered by astonishment. You will not know whether you should be more astonished by the position of Qatadah (DoD: 117 AH), may Allah's mercy be upon him, in relation to this noble Prophetic characteristic? Or be more astonished by this Prophetic characteristic in the midst of this tremendous situation?!

What catches the attention here is that Qatadah (DoD: 117 AH), may Allah's mercy be upon him, was objective and demonstrated his care for the major Quranic aim, which is the refinement of the

---

[140] Tafsir At-Tabari (9/139).

Akhlaq [141]. The counterpart of this verse is the statement of Al-Khaleel (Ibrahim), peace be upon him:

﴿وَمَنْ عَصَانِي فَإِنَّكَ، غَفُورٌ رَّحِيمٌ﴾

"And whoever disobeys me, then verily you are Forgiving and Merciful"
[TMQ Ibrahim: 36]

The following came recorded in the Sahih of Al-Bukhari in relation to the description of the Noble Prophet ﷺ, from Anas, may Allah be pleased with him, who said:

لَمْ يَكُنِ النَّبِيُّ صلى الله عليه وسلم سَبَّابًا وَلاَ فَحَّاشًا وَلاَ لَعَّانًا، كَانَ يَقُولُ لأَحَدِنَا عِنْدَ الْمَعْتَبَةِ: مَا لَهُ، تَرِبَ جَبِينُهُ

The Prophet ﷺ was not one who **would insult, say obscene words, or curse (others),** and if he wanted to admonish anyone of us, he used to say: **"What is wrong with him, (let) his forehead be dusted!"** [142].

This is sufficient for you as evidence as Anas, may Allah be pleased with him, was his servant for ten years, and the moral character of a person with servants and those like them is more telling than that with those whom the person seeks a benefit from. This tradition encourages those calling to Islam and the reformers to be upon the methodology of the Messengers in terms of mercy, manners, moral character and kindness, and with that the impact will be greater and the blessing will be more encompassing.

---

[141] Refer to: Tafsir Ibn 'Aashour (1/40).
[142] Al-Bukhari, Book of *Al-Adab*, chapter: The Messenger ﷺ did not use obscene language, Hadith number (6031).

The Messengers, who are the best of creation, teach mankind the correct manner of how to conduct themselves with Allah and how their manners should be with Him تعالى:

﴿أُولَٰئِكَ الَّذِينَ هَدَى اللَّهُ ۖ فَبِهُدَاهُمُ اقْتَدِهْ﴾

"They are those whom Allah had guided. So, emulate their guidance"

[TMQ Al-An'am: 90]

Zeal and passion for the *Deen* of Allah is not a justification for using obscene and foul language or defaming others. We do not have more zeal for the *Deen* of Allah than the Prophets of Allah تعالى and there is a difference between the one who seeks victory for Allah and the one who seeks triumph for himself. The one who seeks victory for Allah never resorts to vulgarity regardless of how much the manners of his opponent descend into vulgarity. That is because:

لَيْسَ الْمُؤْمِنُ بِالطَّعَّانِ، وَلَا اللَّعَّانُ، وَلَا الْفَاحِشَ، وَلَا الْبَذِيءَ

"The believer is not a defamer, a curser (of others), or a user of obscenities and foulness" [143]

---

[143] At-Tirmidhi, Chapters of Al-Birr Wa As-Silah, chapter: What came concerning the cursing, Hadith number (1977). Al-Albani classified it as Sahih in his Silsilat As-Sahihah (1/634).

Projects of Harm and Ruin

Close to the sublime Masjid Quba which was established upon the basis of *Taqwaa* (piety), they established their entity of ruin. On the outside it had the appearance of being a project of good and righteousness but in the inside, it represented evil and corruption.

As hypocrisy extends until the final hour this project (of harm and ruin) has extended and appeared across history in various forms, just as the noble Taabi' Shaqiq bin Salamah (DoD: After 80 AH), may Allah's mercy be upon him, deduced in a reported tradition attributed to him by At-Tabari (DoD: 310 AH), concerning His statement تعالى:

﴿وَالَّذِينَ اتَّخَذُوا مَسْجِدًا ضِرَارًا وَكُفْرًا وَتَفْرِيقًا بَيْنَ الْمُؤْمِنِينَ وَإِرْصَادًا لِّمَنْ حَارَبَ اللَّهَ وَرَسُولَهُ مِن قَبْلُ﴾

"And [there are] those [hypocrites] who took for themselves a mosque for causing harm and disbelief and division among the believers and as a station for whoever had warred against Allah and His Messenger before"
[TMQ At-Tawbah: 107]

He said:

كلُّ مسجدٍ بُنِيَ ضِرارًا أو رياءً أو سمعةً، فإن أصلَه ينتهي إلى المسجد الذي بُنِيَ ضِرَارًا

"Every Masjid (mosque) built for the purpose of harm, hypocrisy (by making a show in front of people) or seeking reputation (and standing), then its origin goes back to the Masjid that was built for the purpose of causing harm** (i.e. Masjid Ad-*Diraar*)" [144]

Here we read something from the secret of the Qur'an's eternalization of the first project of harm and ruin: Masjid Ad-*Diraar*. That is because it represents an origin as mentioned by Shaqiq (DoD: After 80 AH), may Allah's mercy be upon him, and from it there will be an extension and branches that manifest. This reflects the light of insight which Allah bestows upon the companion of the Qur'an, to be able to look to the future in accordance with the telescope of *Iman* and the insight of the heart.

This Qur'anic cautioning and this deduction from the Salaf (righteous predecessor) concerning the danger of harmful projects and those behind them upon the societies, prompted Al-Imam Ibn ul-Qayyim (DoD: 751 AH) to say:

كادَ القرآن أن يكون كله في شأنهم؛ لكثرتهم على ظهر الأرض وفي أجواف القبور

"It is almost as if the Qur'an as a whole is related to them (i.e. the hypocrites), due to their large number upon the face of the earth and the insides of the graves" [145]

Yes, the first Masjid Ad-*Diraar* was demolished, however its branches disperse their poison and spread their filth. They manifest in numerous activities which are apparently in support of Islam whilst in reality they seek to distort the eternal image of Islam. They manifest as: Conferences of *Diraar* (harm), books of *Diraar* and research (or studies) of *Diraar*! The means have differed, but the aim remains one and the same!

---

[144] Tafsir At-Tabari (11/680).
[145] Madaarij As-Saalikeen (1/364).

They are newly occurring projects employing various means which continue to arise in every age and in a variety of flavours.

Every project of harm has fundamental constituent parts and elements, which Masjid Ad-*Diraar* shares with the forums of harm or conferences of harm. There are two constant permanent fundamental elements which do not differ or change with the passing of time and are not hidden from the one whom Allah has illuminated his sight and radiated his heart with the verses of His Book. These two fundamental elements are constituted as follows:

1. The harmful intended aim: When the aim is illegitimate and is to bring harm to the *Deen* of Allah or the Muslims, then it is a project of *Diraar* (harm and ruin). That is even if it was in the form of the most beloved spot to Allah: "The Masjid".

2. The underhanded pollution: That is where its appearance is that of a project, like all of the projects of harm through the ages of the Ummah, which is used as a cover in order to accomplish an underhanded objective or purpose.

Based upon these two constituting elements we are able to determine the projects of harm: **That they are *Deeni* (religious) projects whilst behind them there is an illegitimate purpose, which is to distort the correct and just Islamic *Deen*.** Any project containing these two constituent elements is an illegitimate project and must be warned about. That is because Allah تعالى does not accept actions except those which are sincere and seek that which is correct. Ibn ul-Qayyim (DoD: 751 AH) said:

"The insincere hypocritical intentions of those involved in hypocrisy made Masjid Ad-*Diraar* a dunghill and place of ruin which you would not stand in ever, whilst the sincerity of the sincere elevated the status of the Tafath (unclean elements or hair attached to the body)] [146] (Translator's Note: This is a reference to the acts of Hajj and the cutting of nails and trimming or plucking of hair etc.).

In this captivating statement, he, may Allah's mercy be upon him, presents the true measure of the action, and its standing before Allah based upon what is in the hearts and not based upon the quantity or the how. Sincerity raises the status of the Tafath where the Tafath relates to taking from the bodily hair in the rituals of Hajj. It is as if he is alluding to Allah's mention of it in His speech تعالى:

﴿﴿ ثُمَّ لْيَقْضُوا تَفَثَهُمْ وَلْيُوفُوا نُذُورَهُمْ وَلْيَطَّوَّفُوا بِالْبَيْتِ الْعَتِيقِ﴾﴾

"Then let them end their untidiness and fulfil their vows and perform Tawaf around the ancient House"   [TMQ Al-Hajj: 29]

Here, he is demonstrating that the importance is not in the hugeness of the projects but rather lies in their root origins and aims (or intended purposes).

The best one to explain this statement of his is himself, where he, may Allah's mercy be upon him, says in another place: [The intention is the head of the matter, its pillar, basis and its origin upon which it is built. That is because it is the spirit of the action, its benefit and motive. That action is its consequence and is established upon it. It is correct by its correctness and corrupted by its corruption. Through it *Tawfiq* is attained whilst with its absence abandonment occurs. In accordance with it the grades in the *Dunyaa* (life of this world) and *Akhirah* (hereafter) differ" [147]

Therefore, O Believer! There are only two kinds of project and no third: Either the project of *Taqwaa* (piety) or the project of *Diraar*

---

[146] Badaa'i Al-Fawaa'id, Ibn ul-Qayyim (3/237).
[147] A'alaam Al-Muwaqqi'een, Ibn ul-Qayyim (6/106).

(harm and ruin). That is whilst it is the intended aims and purposes which are the determining factor. That is as there is a vast difference between that which is founded upon the basis of *Taqwaa* and that which is founded upon Idraar (to bring harm) with the intention to exploit to attack. May Allah protect us from corruption and its causes.

The Complete Woman

When a woman challenges the most tyrannically oppressive man and the most powerful kingdom; a single woman in the face of the greatest empire of the time! Can you imagine, O honourable brother, such a confrontation?! Indeed, she was not just any woman but rather his wife as well! However, despite that she did not care for the customs of the people! She did not give in to the pressures of the society and did not compromise before the fineries of the palace and the show of the life of pomp and splendour! This is the spirit when it is attached to Allah. It seeks to make easy every difficult matter in the way of the *Deen* and the belief.

Al-Imam At-Tabari (DoD: 310 AH) attributed to Qatadah (DoD: 117 AH), may Allah's mercy be upon him, concerning the statement of Allah تعالى:

﴿وَضَرَبَ اللَّهُ مَثَلًا لِّلَّذِينَ آمَنُوا امْرَأَتَ فِرْعَوْنَ إِذْ قَالَتْ رَبِّ ابْنِ لِي عِندَكَ بَيْتًا فِي الْجَنَّةِ وَنَجِّنِي مِن فِرْعَوْنَ وَعَمَلِهِ وَنَجِّنِي مِنَ الْقَوْمِ الظَّالِمِينَ﴾

"*And Allah presents an example of those who believed: The wife of Pharaoh, when she said: "My Lord, build for me near You a house in Paradise and save me from Pharaoh and his deeds and save me from the wrongdoing people*"   [TMQ At-Tahrim: 11]

That he said:

وكان أعتى أهل الأرض على الله، وأبعده من الله، فوالله ما ضر امرأته كفر زوجها حين أطاعت ربها، لتعلموا أن الله حَكَمٌ عدل، لا يؤاخذ عبده إلا بذنبه

"He was the most tyrannically oppressive of the people of the earth at that time and the furthest away from Allah. By Allah, his wife was not harmed by the Kufr (disbelief) of her husband when she obeyed her *Rabb* (Lord). That is for you to know that Allah is a just Hakam (judge) and does not take His slave to task (or account) except for his own sin" [148]

This is how the stories of the Qur'an should be read in a manner that seeks to attain what they intend to impart. It is from this that Qatadah (DoD: 117 AH), may Allah's mercy be upon him, deduced this guidance linked to *Iman*. In this reported tradition attributed to him we find a severing of the ambitions of those who are disobedient who hope to gain benefit from the uprightness of their relations. That is as there is no bond stronger than that of sonhood, fatherhood and wifehood. The wife of Fir'awn (Pharaoh) was not harmed by the corruption of her husband, just as was the case of Ibrahim with his father and Nuh with his wife and son. That is just as Allah تعالى said to his Prophet ﷺ:

﴿إِنَّكَ لَا تَهْدِي مَنْ أَحْبَبْتَ وَلَٰكِنَّ اللَّهَ يَهْدِي مَن يَشَاءُ ۚ وَهُوَ أَعْلَمُ بِالْمُهْتَدِينَ﴾

---

[148] Tafsir At-Tabari (23/115-116).

"Indeed, [O Muhammad], you do not guide whom you like, but Allah guides whom He wills. And He is most knowing of the [rightly] guided"
[TMQ Al-Qasas: 56] [149]

This can be a cause for the spread of corruption in the Ummah: Dependence upon the uprightness of the close relation. That is because it reflects an important aspect of great impact linked to the *Iman* in relation to the life of the Ummah. This cause, however, has reached a dangerous turn in the minds of the people as they have fabricated Ahadeeth related to it. For this reason, Ibn Kathir (DoD: 774 AH) said in the Tafsir of the verse:

استدل بهذه الآية الكريمة بعض العلماء على ضعف الحديث الذي يأثره كثير من الناس: من أكل مع مغفور له غفر له. وهذا الحديث لا أصل له، وإنما يُروى هذا عن بعض الصالحين أنه رأى النبي في المنام فقال: يا رسول الله، أنت قلت: من أكل مع مغفور له غفر؟ قال: لا، ولكني الآن أقوله

"Some of the *'Ulamaa'* (Scholars) deduced from this noble verse the weakness of the Hadith which many of the people narrate: "Whoever eats with the one who is forgiven is forgiven". This Hadith as no basis for it. This was only related from some of the righteous, that he saw the Prophet ﷺ whilst dreaming and he said: "O Messenger of Allah. Did you say: "Whoever eats with the one who is forgiven, is forgiven?" He said: "No, but now I say it" [150]

This cause was not restricted to the corruption of the *Deen* of the Ummah but is badness extended and became a cause for the falling behind of the Ummah in her *Dunyaa* (worldly life) until

---

[149] Refer to: Tafsir Ath-Tha'labi (27/64) and Tafsir Al-Baghawi (5/123).

[150] Tafsir Ibn Kathir (8/171).

unemployment spread and the love for indifference and recreation, leaning upon the great feats of the ancestors and binding themselves to their past standings and uprightness.

It also severs despair from the reformers and righteous, in respect to the sinful acts of disobedience of others not harming them when they engage in acts of obedience and perform what is obliged upon them in terms of commanding the *Ma'roof* and forbidding the *Munkar*, when they are capable of that [151]. If Allah does not take to task the slave except by his own sin, then that dictates that we do not pass judgement upon people by the crimes of their fathers, brothers or tribes.

This loftiness demonstrated by the wife of Fir'awn and eternalized by the Qur'an represents an invitation to them to hold firm to obedience and be steadfast upon the *Deen*. That is especially the case in the time of strangeness, as a believing woman could exist among a nation of disbelievers, or a righteous woman could exist within a depraved or wicked house and so on.

Al-Qurtubi (DoD: 671 AH), may Allah's mercy be upon him, said:

وقيل: هذا حث للمؤمنين على الصبر في الشدة، أي: لا تكونوا في الصبر عند الشدة أضعف من امرأة فرعون حين صبرت على أذى فرعون

"And it has been said: This is an encouragement for the believers to persevere patiently at the time of difficulty (or hardship). It means: Do not be weaker in your patient perseverance at the time

---

of hardship than the wife of Fir'awn when she patiently persevered in the face of the harm of Fir'awn" [152]

And it is important that you know O male and female believer, that seeking refuge in Allah تعالى at the time of trials and asking Him for relief from it, is from the Sunan (ways) of the righteous servants and the Prophets, as Abu Hayyan (DoD: 745 AH) mentioned in his Tafsir. [153]

It is true what he said, as how could this weak woman stand steadfast with Allah in the face of the biggest and most arrogant tyrant upon the earth, had it not been for her seeking refuge in Allah:

﴿وَضَرَبَ اللَّهُ مَثَلًا لِّلَّذِينَ آمَنُوا امْرَأَتَ فِرْعَوْنَ إِذْ قَالَتْ رَبِّ ابْنِ لِي عِندَكَ بَيْتًا فِي الْجَنَّةِ وَنَجِّنِي مِن فِرْعَوْنَ وَعَمَلِهِ وَنَجِّنِي مِنَ الْقَوْمِ الظَّالِمِينَ﴾

"And Allah presents an example of those who believed: The wife of Pharaoh, when she said, "My Lord, build for me near You a house in Paradise and save me from Pharaoh and his deeds and save me from the wrongdoing people"   [TMQ At-Tahrim: 11]

How could she not feel hopeless in such a major trial, the like of which the people of minds of reason and dreams would lose hope in?!

Contemplate when the trial encompassed the Prophet of Allah Yusuf, peace be upon him, and the key to relief and escape for him was:

---

[152] Tafsir Al-Qurtubi (18/202/203).
[153] Refer to: Tafsir Abu Hayyan (10/216).

﴿قَالَ رَبِّ السِّجْنُ أَحَبُّ إِلَيَّ مِمَّا يَدْعُونَنِي إِلَيْهِۖ وَإِلَّا تَصْرِفْ عَنِّي كَيْدَهُنَّ أَصْبُ إِلَيْهِنَّ وَأَكُن مِّنَ الْجَاهِلِينَ﴾

"He said: "My Lord, prison is more beloved to me than that which they invite me to. And if You do not avert from me their plan, I might incline toward them and [thus] become of the ignorant"   [TMQ Yusuf: 33]

The key difference between consistency and inconsistency is the *Du'aa* and asking for relief. The one who remained firm only did so due to the sincerity of his seeking refuge with Allah تعالى and the one who rode the wave only did so due to his reliance upon himself and Allah تعالى. Allah's judgement is just and He does not take to task His slave except for the sin that he committed as indicated to by Qatadah in the beautiful tradition linked to the *Iman*.

Through this lofty firm perseverance this woman attained the greatest Prophetic honour which is the Prophetic praise upon her with Kamaal (completion or perfection) which came stated in the Hadith related by Abu Musa Al-Ash'ari, may Allah be pleased with him:

كَمَلَ مِنَ الرِّجَالِ كَثِيرٌ، وَلَمْ يَكْمُلْ مِنَ النِّسَاءِ إِلاَّ مَرْيَمُ بِنْتُ عِمْرَانَ، وَآسِيَةُ امْرَأَةُ فِرْعَوْنَ

Many amongst men attained perfection but amongst women none attained the perfection except Maryam, the daughter of `Imran and Aasiyah, the wife of Fir'awn (Pharaoh) [154]

---

[154] Al-Bukhari, Book of foodstuffs, chapter of Ath-Thareed, Hadith number (5418). Muslim, Book of Fadaa'il, chapter of the Fadaa'il of Khadijah the Mother of Believers, may Allah be pleased with her, Hadith number: 2431).

As such, may Allah be pleased with every woman who has remained patient and persevered, and who strived earnestly and expended her effort in the way of the Aqeedah (belief), the *Deen*, knowledge and teaching. The one who was a righteous example in her house, surroundings and society. That is the perfection that is sought and the success that is forthcoming.

What will make you comprehend the meaning of taking the Qur'an as a pillow?!

In the quietness of the night and its stillness a new life of the believer is renewed, when the trivialities of feelings and preoccupations are dispelled from his *Rooh* (spirit), for it to obtain the true provision for the exhausting journey of life.

As the Qur'an Al-'Azheem represents the light in that life, its companion is entitled to the special characteristics, rulings, favouring and blessings which do not come to others.

Al-Imam At-Tabari (DoD: 310 AH) attributed to Abu Rajaa' Al-Basri, may Allah's mercy be upon him, that he said concerning His statement تعالى:

$$﴿فَاقْرَءُوا مَا تَيَسَّرَ مِنَ الْقُرْآنِ﴾$$

"So, recite what is easy [for you] of the Qur'an"

[TMQ Al-Muzzammil: 20]

قلتُ للحسن البصري [ت: 110]: يا أبا سعيد! ما تقولُ في رجلٍ قد اسْتَظْهَر القرآنَ كلَّه عن ظهرِ قلبِه، فلا يقومُ به، إنما يُصَلِّي المكتوبة؟ قال: يتَوَسَّدُ القرآن! لعن اللهُ ذاك، قال اللهُ جلَّ ذكره للعبدِ الصالح

"I said to Al-Hasan Al-Basri (DoD: 110 AH): "O Abu Sa'eed! What do you say concerning a man who has memorized the whole Qur'an by heart, but does not stand in prayer with it (i.e. night prayer) and only prays the obligatory prayers?" He said: He has made the

Qur'an like a pillow [155] Allah curses that. Allah, majestic is His mention, said to the righteous slave:

$$﴿وَإِنَّهُ لَذُو عِلْمٍ لِّمَا عَلَّمْنَاهُ﴾$$

"And indeed, he was a possessor of knowledge because of what We had taught him" [TMQ Yusuf: 68]

$$﴿وَعُلِّمْتُم مَّا لَمْ تَعْلَمُوا أَنتُمْ وَلَا آبَاؤُكُمْ﴾$$

"And you were taught that which you knew not, neither you nor your fathers" [TMQ Al-An'am: 91]

I said: "O Abu Sa'id, Allah said:

$$﴿فَاقْرَءُوا مَا تَيَسَّرَ مِنَ الْقُرْآنِ﴾$$

"So, recite what is easy [for you] of the Qur'an" [TMQ Al-Muzzammil: 20]

He said: "Yes, even if (only) fifty verses] [156]

The wisdom of this tradition in respect to his statement "They make the Qur'an like a pillow" appears in the clarification of Al-Imam Ibn Kathir (DoD: 774), when he said after quoting the tradition:

وهذا ظاهرٌ من مذهب الحسن البصري: أنه كان يرى حقًّا واجبًا على حملة القرآن

أن يقوموا ولو بشيء منه في الليل

---

[155] The meaning of this is: That he sleeps and does not recite the Qur'an whilst he has memorised it. When he spleeps he has nothing with him from the Qur'an.

[156] Tafsir At-Tabari (33/396).

"This is apparent from the *Madh'hab* (views) of Al-Hasan Al-Basri, that he viewed it to be an obligatory right upon the carrier (or possessor) of the Qur'an to stand in prayer, even with some of it, during the night" [157]

The blessing of the Qur'an obliges gratitude, and this is apparent from his deduction from the statement of Allah تعالى:

﴿وَعُلِّمْتُم مَّا لَمْ تَعْلَمُوا أَنتُمْ وَلَا آبَاؤُكُمْ﴾

"And you were taught that which you knew not, neither you nor your fathers" [TMQ Al-An'am: 91]

Gratitude for the blessing of the Qur'an is manifested by acting by it and that is from his deduction, may Allah's mercy be upon him, with the statement of Allah تعالى:

﴿وَإِنَّهُ لَذُو عِلْمٍ لِّمَا عَلَّمْنَاهُ﴾

"And indeed, he was a possessor of knowledge because of what We had taught him" [TMQ Yusuf: 68]

In this context, it means: Acting by the Qur'an Al-Karim.

Acting by the Qur'an includes: Standing in prayer with it during the middle of the night, which is understood from his words:

يتوسَّد القرآن

"He has made the Qur'an like a pillow"

 Its meaning in this context is one of censure. It is as if the memorization of the Qur'an, in the view of Al-Hasan AL-Basri, is not worth anything unless the person stands in prayer with it

---

[157] Tafsir Ibn Kathir (8/259).

during the heart of the night and acts in accordance with it during the day. That is because the Qur'an only intercedes for the one who stands in prayer with it as Ibn Rajab (DoD: 795 AH), Allah's mercy be upon him, said [158].

Allah تعالى said in relation to the Ahl ul-*Kitab* (People of the Book):

﴿قُلْ يَا أَهْلَ الْكِتَابِ لَسْتُمْ عَلَىٰ شَيْءٍ حَتَّىٰ تُقِيمُوا التَّوْرَاةَ وَالْإِنجِيلَ وَمَا أُنزِلَ إِلَيْكُم مِّن رَّبِّكُمْ ۗ وَلَيَزِيدَنَّ كَثِيرًا مِّنْهُم مَّا أُنزِلَ إِلَيْكَ مِن رَّبِّكَ طُغْيَانًا وَكُفْرًا ۖ فَلَا تَأْسَ عَلَى الْقَوْمِ الْكَافِرِينَ﴾

"Say: "O People of the Book, you are [standing] on nothing until you establish [the law of] the Tawrah, the Injeel, and what has been revealed to you from your Lord". And that which has been revealed to you from your Lord will surely increase many of them in transgression and disbelief. So do not grieve over the disbelievers"   [TMQ Al-Ma'idah: 68]

The greatest establishing of the Qur'an is standing with it in the middle of the night and acting in accordance with it.

This reported tradition in truth, is in completely harmony with the understanding of Al-Hasan (DoD: 110 AH), may Allah's mercy be upon him, concerning the *Tadabbur* (deep thought and contemplation). That is when he said:

وما تدبُّر آياتِه إلا اتباعُه بعلمِه، والله ما هو بحفظ حروفه وإضاعة حدوده، حتى أن أحدهم ليقول: والله لقد قرأتُ القرآنَ كلَّه وما أسقط منه حرفًا واحدًا وقد أسقطه كله، ما ترى له في القرآن من خلق ولا عمل!

---

158 Refer to: Lataa'if Al-Ma'aarif, Ibn Rajab (p 172).

"The *Tadabbur* (deep thought and contemplation) of its verses does not mean except following it by its knowledge. By Allah, it is not by the memorization of its letters but neglecting its limits, where one of them would say: By Allah, I have read the Qur'an in its entirety and I have not dropped one letter from it, whilst he had (in reality) dropped all of it, as nothing of the Qur'an is seen in his moral character and action!" [159].

The reader of the Qur'an becomes aware of its majesty when he knows that the *Ameer ul-Mu'mineen* (Leader of Believers) Uthman bin 'Affaan, may Allah be pleased with him, despite the burdens of the Khilafah and the huge number of his assignments, did not allow them to be a reason to permit leaving the night prayer.

Indeed, his wife said on the day of the house (i.e. when his home was besieged):

اقتلوه أو دعوه فوالله لقد كان يحيي الليل بالقرآن في ركعة

"Kill him or leave him, as by Allah he used to spend the whole night with the Qur'an in one Rak'ah (unit of prayer)" [160]. How could this not be his condition whilst he was the one who strove his utmost to compile the Qur'an Al-Karim? And how could this not be his condition when it was he who said:

لو أن قلوبَنا طَهُرَت ما شبعنا من كلام ربنا

"Even if our hearts became purified, we would never tire (or had enough) of the speech of our *Rabb* (Lord)"[161]

---

[159] Musannaf Abdur Razzaq, book of Fadaa'il Al-Qur'an, chapter of Ta'aahud Al-Qur'an (3/363).
[160] Al-Bidayah Wa-n-Nihayah, Ibn Kathir (7/217).
[161] Same source as above (7/217).

Uthman was not unique in this divine methodology, rather, this was the condition of all of them. Al-Hasan bin 'Ali, may Allah be pleased with him, said:

إن من كان قبلكم رأوا القرآن رسائل من ربهم فكانوا يتدبرونها بالليل ويتفقدونها في النهار

"Those who came before you saw the Qur'an as messages from their *Rabb* (Lord). So, they used to contemplate it during the night and review it (ppractically during the day" [162].

Reflect with me O blessed one, the secret of the linkage between the action of the night and the action of the day. That is because the standing of prayer at night has an impact in respect to the action during the day, just as *Ihsaan* (perfection) in respect to worshipping Allah reflects upon the good moral character of the person with the people.

Maintaining that is the advice of our Prophet ﷺ to the people of the Qur'an when he said in the famous Hadith which was related by 'Ali bin Abi Talib, may Allah be pleased with him:

يَا أَهْلَ الْقُرْآنِ أَوْتِرُوا فَإِنَّ اللَّهَ وِتْرٌ يُحِبُّ الْوِتْرَ

"O people of the Qur'an! Offer Witr (prayer), because Allah is Witr (One) and loves Witr" [163].

---

[162] At-Tibyaan Fee Aadaab Hamlat ul-Qur'an, An-Nawawi (p 54).

[163] Abu Dawud, Book of Salaah (prayer)m chapter: Tafree' Abwaab ul-Witr, Hadith number (1416). At-Tirmidhi, Chapters of Al-Witr, chapter of what came in relation to the Witr not being obligatory, Hadith number (453). He said: [The Hadith of 'Ali is a Hasan Hadith]. Ibn Maajah, the Book of the establishment of the prayer, the chapter of what came in relation to Al-Witr, Hadith number

Verily, the verse of Al-Muzzammil:

$$﴿فَاقْرَءُوا مَا تَيَسَّرَ مِنَ الْقُرْآنِ﴾$$

"So, recite what is easy [for you] of the Qur'an"   [TMQ Al-Muzzammil: 20]

In addition to the above reported tradition of Al-Hasan Al-Basri (DoD: 110 AH) and the verses urging the prayer during the night in general, radiate in the heart of the companion of the Qur'an and call to him (saying) that Allah تعالى has chosen you with a great blessing which makes others envious of you.

And Allah addresses you with standing during the night in prayer in a manner that he did not address other than you [164]. Affiliation to the Qur'an requires clear evidence or otherwise, it would just be a claim. The greatest evidence is the action with the Qur'an, and the greatest from that is: Standing with it in the heart of the night. So glad tidings to those who are devoutly obedient, prostrating through the night fearing the hereafter and hoping for the mercy of their *Rabb* (Lord).

I seek refuge in Allah from the cast out *Shaytan* (Satan):

$$﴿أَمَّنْ هُوَ قَانِتٌ آنَاءَ اللَّيْلِ سَاجِدًا وَقَائِمًا يَحْذَرُ الْآخِرَةَ وَيَرْجُو رَحْمَةَ رَبِّهِ قُلْ هَلْ يَسْتَوِي الَّذِينَ يَعْلَمُونَ وَالَّذِينَ لَا يَعْلَمُونَ إِنَّمَا يَتَذَكَّرُ أُولُو الْأَلْبَابِ﴾$$

"Is one who is devoutly obedient during periods of the night, prostrating and standing [in prayer], fearing the Hereafter and hoping for the mercy of his Lord, [like one who does not]? Say: "Are those who know equal to

---

(1169. Al-Albani classified it as Hasan in Sahih Al-Jaami' As-Sagheer Wa Ziyaadatuhu (1/375).

[164] Refer to: Majmoo' Fataawaa, Sheikh ul-Islam Ibn Taymiyah (23/84).

those who do not know?" Only those [who are] people of understanding will remember" [TMQ Az-Zumar: 9]

Is there a seeker of knowledge so that he can be assisted upon it?!

The souls yearned for the land of Al-Kinanah (Egypt) in the pursuit of knowledge. They traveled to it from the east of the Islamic world, and that is why Egypt had a rendezvous with the major *'Ulamaa'* (scholars) of the *Deen*. Muhammad bin Jarir At-Tabari (DoD: 310 AH), Muhammad bin Ishaq bin Khuzaimah (DoD: 311 AH), Muhammad bin Harun Ar-Ruyani (DoD: 307 AH) and Muhammad bin Nasr Al-Marwazi (DoD: 294 AH) all headed towards it in the pursuit of knowledge, which is the most valuable pursuit and most valued goal. It was in Egypt that the story was told.

Their food ran out, and this noble congregation became hungry. Their grief accumulated as they were deprived of their families, homeland, and needs.

The honourable masters met together in one of the houses hungry, far from their homelands and perplexed. It is like their circumstances were like those illustrated by Ibn 'Abbas in respect to the situation of Musa, peace be upon him, in relation to His statement تعالى:

$$﴿فَسَقَىٰ لَهُمَا ثُمَّ تَوَلَّىٰ إِلَى الظِّلِّ فَقَالَ رَبِّ إِنِّي لِمَا أَنزَلْتَ إِلَيَّ مِنْ خَيْرٍ فَقِيرٌ﴾$$

"So, he watered for them; then he went back to the shade and said: My Lord, indeed I am, for whatever good You would send down to me, in need"
[TMQ Al-Qasas: 24]

Ibn 'Atiyah (DoD: 542 AH) transmitted the following statement of Ibn 'Abbas, may Allah be pleased with them both:

وكان قد بلغ به الجوع واخضر لونه من أكل البقل، وضعف حتى لصق بطنه بظهره، ورُئيتَ خضرة البقل في بطنه، وإنه لأكرم الخلق يومئذ على الله

"His hunger had reached the extent that his complexion had turned green from eating the green herbs and plants and he became weak to the extent that his stomach was stuck to his back and the green of the herbage (or plants) was visible in his stomach. That is whilst he was the most honourable of the creation in the sight of Allah at that time". Ibn 'Atiyah (DoD: 542 AH) added:

ورُوِي أنه لم يصل إلى مَدْين حتى سقط باطن قدمه، وفي هذا معتبر وحاكم بهوان الدنيا على الله تعالى

"It has been related that he did not reach Madyan until the soles of his feet had peeled (off). **In this there is a point for consideration and a judgement in respect to the insignificance of the *Dunyaa* in the sight of Allah تعالى** [165]. And those *'Ulamaa'* were following the path of the Prophets.

Their hunger reached the extent that they would draw lots where the one who pulled the lot would ask others on their behalf. That is whilst they were the nobles among their people and well known within their societies. However, it was the estrangement and hunger which Muhammad ﷺ sought refuge in Allah from that led them to this, when he said:

اللَّهُمَّ إِنِّي أَعُوذُ بِكَ مِنَ الْجُوعِ فَإِنَّهُ بِئْسَ الضَّجِيعُ

---

[165] Tafsir Ibn 'Atiyah (4/284).

"O Allah, I seek refuge in You from hunger, for it is the worst companion" [166]

The lot fell to Al-Imam Muhammad bin Khuzaimah (DoD: 311); however, their inner selves had too much honor to ask for anything from other than Allah تعالى. So, he said:

يسأل: أيكم محمد بن نصر؟ فقيل: هو ذا، فأخرج صرة فيها خمسون دينارًا، فدفعها إليه، ثم قال: وأيكم محمد بن جرير؟ فأعطاه خمسين دينارًا، وكذلك للروياني، وابن خزيمة،

"Give me some time until I have prayed!" Then whilst he was praying, busy in supplication and asking Allah for a relief to come! The door was knocked upon and it was the envoy of the Ameer (leader). They opened the door to him and he asked: "Which of you is Muhammad bin Nasr?" It was said: "This is him". He then took out a purse containing 50 *Deenar* and he gave it to him. He then said: "And which of you is Muhammad bin Jarir?" He then gave him 50 *Deenar* and then he did the same with Ar-Ruyani and Ibn Khuzaimah.

He then said:

---

[166] Abu Dawud, chapter Tafree' Abwaab ul-Witr, chapter related to Al-Isti'aadhah, Hadith number (1547). An-Nasa'i in the book of Al-Isti'aadhah (seeking refuge in Allah), Seeking refuge from hunger, Hadith number (5468). Ibn Maajah. Book of foodstuffs, the chapter of seeking refuge from hunger, Hadith number (3354). Al-Albani classified it as Hasan in his Sahih At-Targheeb Wa t-Tarheeb (3/155).

إن الأمير كان قائلًا بالأمس، فرأى في المنام أن المحامد [جامع اسم هؤلاء الأربعة]

جياع قد طووا كشحهم فأنفذ إليكم هذه الصرر، وأقسم عليكم: إذا نفدت،

فابعثوا إليّ أحدكم

"Indeed, the Amir was saying yesterday, as he had seen in his dream that the four Muhammads were hungry and were keeping it secret. So, (he said): "I give to you these purses (of money) and swear to you that if it runs out, then let one of you send to me" [167].

The wonder here, O blessed brother, is that one of those scholars was Al-Imam At-Tabari (DoD: 310 AH), may Allah's mercy be upon him, a central figure of our radiances in this book and one of our sources for these radiant reported traditions of those noble, righteous predecessors (*Salaf*) and their living with the verses of the *Kitab* (Al-Qur'an) and its secrets. It was he, may Allah's mercy be upon him, who attributed to Matar Al-Warraq (DoD: 129 AH) concerning His statement تعالى:

$$﴿وَلَقَدْ يَسَّرْنَا الْقُرْآنَ لِلذِّكْرِ فَهَلْ مِن مُّدَّكِرٍ﴾$$

"And We have indeed made the Qur'an easy for remembrance, so is there any who will remember?"   [TMQ Al-Qamar: 17]

That he said:

هلْ مِنْ طَالِبِ علم فيُعَان عليه؟!

---

[167] It was mentioned by Al-Khateeb Al-Baghdadi in "Tareekh Al-Baghdad" (2/548), Ibn 'Asakir in "Tareekh Dimashq" (52/193), Al-Hamawi in "Mu'jam Al-Udabaa'" (6/2445) and Adh-Dhahabi in "Siyar Al-A'alam An-Nubala'" (14/270-271).

"Is there a seeker of knowledge so that he can be assisted upon it?!" [168].

The seeker of knowledge is deserving of this divine assistance as knowledge is acquired only through toil and exertion, while the best of actions are those which are most resolute [169]. Consequently, whoever bears the hardship in its pursuit is assisted by Allah and included in the help of Allah for him is the facilitating of the means to attain Al-Jannah (Paradise).

That is like what came stated in the Hadith:

مَنْ سَلَكَ طَرِيقًا يَطْلُبُ فِيهِ عِلْمًا سَلَكَ اللَّهُ بِهِ طَرِيقًا مِنْ طُرُقِ الْجَنَّةِ

Whoever treads a path in which he seeks knowledge, Allah will take him on a path from the paths of Jannah (paradise) [170].

At-Tayyibi (DoD: 743 AH) said:

"The indefinite is used here (i.e. in the Hadith) due to their (i.e. the paths) numerosity and variety, meaning that it is caused by a cause whatever the cause is, in terms of leaving homelands, traveling in the lands, spending in it (its pursuit), learning and teaching, authoring and the exertion involved in all of that, which are too numerous to be counted" [171].

---

[168] Tafsir At-Tabari (22/131).

[169] Refer to: Faid ul-Qadeer, Al-Manawi (6/154).

[170] Abu Dawud, *Kitab Al-'Ilm*, chapter: Encouragement to seek knowledge, Hadith number (3641), At-Tirmidhi, chapters of knowledge, chapter: What came in relation to the virtue of *Fiqh* over worship, Hadith number (2682), Ibn Majah, book introduction, chapter: The virtue of the scholars, Hadith number (223). Related by Abu Ad-Darda', may Allah be pleased with him. Al-Albani classified it as Hasan in his "Sahih At-Targhib Wa t-Tarhib" (1/138).

[171] Sharh Al-Mishkaat, At-Tayyibi (2/666).

The guidance contained in the reported tradition reflects an invitation to the Ummah to seek the knowledge of the Qur'an with seriousness and sincerity whilst removing anxiety from the seekers of knowledge by reminding them of the greatest assistance for them when pursuing the path of knowledge. That is the assistance provided by Allah for them, where there will be assistance on par with the hardship or suffering faced on its path. Consequently, in the case where the pursuit of knowledge is a great and hard pursuit filled with perils and matters which can be unpleasant, Allah's assistance to those upon it is great, and this represents a great incentive for the seeker of knowledge.

These reported traditions have had the greatest impact upon the Ummah, where the journey to seek the knowledge of Tafsir and Hadith became the main headline of the people of knowledge. It is rare to find a scholar who did not travel. Look to the travels of the people of Andalusia and the lands of the East and West to know that this knowledge is precious and that it is not attained by resting the body.

Through the like of this reported tradition, the signs of the verses combine with one another: Hammad bin Zaid (DoD: 179 AH) was asked: ["O Abu Isma'il, has Allah mentioned the people (or scholars) of Hadith in the Qur'an?" He replied: "Yes, have you not heard the speech of Allah تعالى:

﴿وَمَا كَانَ الْمُؤْمِنُونَ لِيَنفِرُوا كَافَّةً ۚ فَلَوْلَا نَفَرَ مِن كُلِّ فِرْقَةٍ مِّنْهُمْ طَائِفَةٌ لِّيَتَفَقَّهُوا فِي الدِّينِ وَلِيُنذِرُوا قَوْمَهُمْ إِذَا رَجَعُوا إِلَيْهِمْ لَعَلَّهُمْ يَحْذَرُونَ﴾

"And it is not for the believers to go out to fight all together. Of every troop of them, a party only should go forth, that they (who are left behind) may

attain understanding in the Deen, and so that they may warn their people when they return to them, so that they may beware"

[TMQ At-Taubah: 122]

This applies to everyone who travels in the pursuit of knowledge and *Fiqh* (understanding) and then returns to those he left behind and then teaches it to them" [172]. How excellent are the ambassadors of the lands: The seekers of knowledge and its people!

Included among the radiances of the story and its lessons is that it demonstrates a practical contemplation for His speech تعالى:

$$﴿وَاسْتَعِينُوا بِالصَّبْرِ وَالصَّلَاةِ﴾$$

"And seek help through patience and prayer"　　　[TMQ Al-Baqarah: 45]

What afflicted the scholars in terms of their provision being exhausted and being estranged from their lands are the trials of the *Dunyaa* for which help is sought via patience and prayer.

If you were to ask O contemplator: **What is the angle of their seeking help by prayer for the trials or calamities of the *Dunyaa*?**

It is said: It includes in it the recitation of the Qur'an, that makes one care little for the *Dunyaa* (worldly life) and seek the *Akhirah* (hereafter). Honoring it provides assistance to the people of obedience to attain earnestness in their efforts. It is like it has been related concerning our Prophet ﷺ that whenever a matter distressed him, he would rush to the prayer [173].

So, know O seeker of knowledge with the certain knowledge that sincerity and striving in worship and extolling the value of the

---

[172] The journey in the pursuit of the Hadith, Al-Khateeb Al-Baghdadi (p 86).
[173] Refer to: Tafsir At-Tabari (1/618).

Qur'an and the prayer, represents the greatest assistance towards understanding the Qur'an and taking delight through cognizance of the 'Ilm (knowledge). And the prayer is the greatest provision for him in the pursuit of knowledge which reflects the path to leadership in the *Deen* and the *Dunyaa* (worldly life):

Abu Bakr, I invited you, if you were to accept

To that which contains your fortune if you understand (well)

To knowledge through which you will be an Imam (leader)

Obeyed if you forbade and if you commanded [174]

O Allah do not obstruct us from the knowledge by an obstruction, and do not prevent us from it by a preventer [175]

---

[174] Diwan Abu Ishaq Al-Ilbeeriy (p 26).
[175] Transmitted by As-Subki from the father of the Imam Al-Haramaini in "Tabaqat Ash-Shafi'iyah Al-Kubra" (5/74).

Seizing the Radiances (*Mashaariq*)

Truthful was the one who said:

إنَّ هذا القرآن لا تفنى عجائبه، ولا تنقضي غرائبه، ولا تنكشف الظلمات إلا به!

"Verily the wonders of this Qur'an have no end, its marvels do not cease and the darknesses are not lifted except by it!" [176].

O honorable reader, the radiances which have preceded are like examples and radiances from the Qur'an Al-Karim, which the *Abd* (slave) takes hold of to enter the world of real life. They are an invitation to complete the journey with the radiances of the verses of Adh-Dhikr ul-Hakim (The Wise Reminder i.e. Al-Qur'an) in the shade of the statements of the *Salaf* (righteous predecessors), for them to be the lantern of life, a project for action and life for the Ummah.

These radiances began with the reported tradition of Mujahid, may Allah's mercy be upon him: [**Drawing the hearts close together!**] That was for the drawing of our hearts close together to be upon the banquet of the Qur'an Al-Karim. They then moved on to address the burdens of sources of distress and anxiety with the reported tradition of Al-Farooq ('Umar), may Allah be pleased with him:

لن يغلب عسر يسرين!

"A hardship will never overcome two eases!"

---

[176] Refer to: Rabee' ul-Abraar, Az-Zamakhshari (2/100).

After that, the journey reached to the matter of kindling the affiliation and belonging to the *Deen* with honour and pride: [**The Entirety of the *Sharee'ah* is Beneficial and for the Well-Being!**]. Then there was a message of advice from the *Salaf* (righteous predecessors) for the pioneers and vanguard of the Ummah, as found under the heading: [**The Soundness of the Role Models and Examples**].

After that, they pruned the *Nafs* (inner self) with the undying statements of Al-Farooq ('Umar), as found in [**The Exhortation of the Distinguished Personalities!**] and then its impact was reaped and its benefit found in [**The Pure Heart and the Hidden (or secret) Voice!**].

Then the radiances rained upon the barrenness of the inner selves (or souls) and dryness of the eyes in: [**The (abundant) Rain of the Hearts!**]. The banner of *Iman* was then raised high and the banner of *Bid'ah* (innovation) was overturned as found in the reported tradition of Sufyan: [**The Companion of every *Bid'ah* (innovation) is Lowly!**].

Just as the ground rejoices with rain, similarly, the hearts of the believers rejoice with the abundant rain of the hearts, as found in: [**Joy with the Qur'an!**]. Then the *Nafs* (inner self / soul) seeks shelter from the blaze and flames of life in *Iman*, as found in: [**The Harbour of Safety!**]. That is where safety and security is found which is absent from fear and distress. The journey continued in this manner with variety and integration alongside the *Sharee'ah* and life. The *Nafs* (inner self) then boarded the boat of salvation through the seeking of knowledge, as found in the invitational call of Matar Al-Warraq: [**Is there a seeker of knowledge so that he can be assisted upon it?!**].

This contribution is an invitation for further deep reflection and contemplation to be undertaken in respect to the signs and verses of Allah تعالى within the universe, selves, revelation and life. It is an invitation to exert effort and strive in respect to the conveyance of the aims of the Qur'an and the illuminations of Adh-Dhikr ul-Hakim (The Wise Reminder i.e. Al-Qur'an) to the entirety of mankind.

It is an invitation for institutional and individual efforts to support one another to correct the concepts and build awareness upon the methodology of the radiances of Adh-Dhikr ul-Hakim (Al-Qur'an).

In conclusion, bringing the points of the Qur'an's guidance closer to comprehension (to the minds and hearts) is an honour to have pride in and service through which one draws near to Allah. Ibn 'Aashour (DoD: 1393), may Allah's mercy be upon him, at the conclusion of his Tafsir when speaking about this honour said:

حقيقٌ بأن يُخدم سعيًا على الرأس!

"It is fitting that an effort serves the one who made it!" [177]

May Allah's mercy be upon the one who assisted by way of advice, correction and guidance. That is as the Muslims are in a good condition as long as they give advice to each other with sincerity.

O Allah, make use of us in obedience to you, make these written sheets blessed for the one who wrote them and the one who reads them. Grant us the good end, make the consequences of our affair good, grant us gratitude that pleases you, good characters which we live with among the people and a mind that we benefit from, O Lord of the worlds.

---

[177] Tafsir Ibn 'Aashour (30/636)

And blessings and peace be upon our Prophet Muhammad and upon his family and companions, altogether.

Sources & References

Al'iitqan Fi ulum AlQuran , Abdalrahman Bin 'Abi Bakr , Jalal Aldiyn Alsuyutii (D: 911 H) , **Editor:** Muhammad 'Abu Alfadl 'Iibrahim , **Publisher:** Alhay'a Almisria Ala'ama Lilkitab , **Edition:** 1394 H-1974 CE.

Al'ahkam Alsultaniah , 'Abu Alhasan Eali Bin Muhamad Bin Muhamad Bin Habib Albasarii Albaghdadi , Also known as Almawardii (Died: 450 H) , **Publisher:** Dar Alhadith , Cairo.

'Ahkam AlQuran , AlQadi Muhamad Bin Abd Allah 'Abu Bakr Almafiri Alashbili Almalikii (Died: 543 H) , **Publisher:** Dar Alkutub Al-Ilmiyah , Beirut , Lebanon , 3rd Edition , 1424 H-2003 CE.

'Iihya' ulum Aldeen , 'Abu Hamid Muhamad Bin Muhamad Alghazali Altusi (Died: 505 H) , **Publisher:** Dar Almaerifa , Beirut.

Al'iikhlas Wan-niya , 'Abu Bakr Abd Allah Bin Muhamad Bin Ubayd Bin Qays Albaghdadii Al'umawii AlQurashii also known as Ibn 'Abi Aldunya (Died: 281 H) , **Edited & Annotated by:** 'Iiad Khalid Altibae , **Publisher:** Dar Albashayir , First Edition , 1413 H.

Al'Adab AlMufrad , Muhamad Bin 'Ismaeil Bin 'Ibrahim Bin Almughira AlBukhari , 'Abu Abdallah (Died: 256 H) , **Edited:** Muhamad Fuad Abdalbaqi , **Publisher:** Dar Albashayir Al'iislamiah , Beirut , 3rd Edition , 1409 H-1989 CE.

Al'Adhkar , 'Abu Zakariaa Muhyi Aldiyn Yahyaa Bin Sharaf Alnawawi (Died: 676 H), **Editor:** Abd Alqadir Al'arnawuwt , **Publisher:** Dar Alfikr Liltiba'at WanNashr WatTawzie , Beirut , Lebanon , 1414 H-1994 CE.

'Iirwa' Alghalil Fi Takhrij 'Ahadith Manar Alsabil , Muhamad Nasir Aldeenn AlAlbanii (Died: 1420 H) , **Supervised by:** Zuhayr

Alshaawish , **Publisher:** Almaktab Al'iislamii Beirut , 2nd Edition 1405 H - 1985 CE.

Al-Istiqamah , Taqi Aldiyn 'Abu AlAbbas 'Ahmad Bin Abd Alhalim Bin Abd Alsalam Bin Taymiah AlHarrani Alhanbali Aldimashqii (Died: 728 H) , **Edited:** Dr. Muhamad Rashad Salim , **Publisher:** JamiAh Al'iimam Muhamad Bin Saud , 1st Edition , 1403 H.

Alaistieab Fi Maerifat Al'ashab , 'Abu Umar Yusuf Bin AbdAllh Bin Muhamad Bin Abd Albirr Bin Asim Alnamrii AlQurtibii (Died: 463 H) , **Edited:** Ali Muhamad Albijawi , **Publisher:** Dar Aljil , Beirut , 1st Edition , 1412 H-1992 CE.

'Alam Almawqien An Rabbi Alalamin , 'Abu AbdAllah , 'Abu Ubayda Mashhur Bin Hasan Al Salman , **Publisher:** Dar Ibn Aljawzi For Publication and Distribution, KSA, 1st Edition , 1423 H

Al'amr Bilmaruf WanNahy An Almunkar , Taqi Aldiyn 'Abu AlAbbaas 'Ahmad Bin Abd Alhalim Bin Abd Alsalam Bin AbdAllah 'Abi Alqasim Bin Muhamad Bin Taymiah AlHarraanii Alhanbali Aldimashqii (Died: 728 H) , **Publisher:** The Ministry for Islamic affairs and endowments, KSA, 1st Edition , 1418 H.

Al'awayil , 'Abu Hilal Alhasan , **Publisher:** Dar Albashir , Tanta , 1st Edition , 1408 H.

Albidayah Walnihayah , 'Abu Alfidaa 'Iismaeil Bin umar Bin Kathir AlQurashii Albasri Thuma Aldimashqi (Died: 774 H) , **Editor:** Abdallah Bin Abdalmuhsin Alturki , **Publisher:** Dar Hajr For Publishing & Distribution & Advertisment,1st Edition 1418 H-1997 CE , **Year of Publishing:** 1424 H-2003 CE.

Badayi' Alfawayid , Dar Alkitaab AlArabi , Beirut , Lebanon.

Alburhan Fi ulum AlQuran , 'Abu Abdallah Badr Aldeen Muhamad Bin Abdallah Bin Bahadur Alzarkashii (Died: 794 H) , **Editor:**

Muhamad 'Abu Alfadl 'Iibrahim , 1st Edition , 1376 H-1957 CE , **Publisher:** Dar 'Iihya' Alkutub Alarabia Eisaa Albabi Alhalabi and Partners.

Albinaya Sharh Alhidaya, 'Abu Muhamad Mahmud Bin 'Ahmad Bin Musaa Bin 'Ahmad Bin Husayn Alghitabi Alhanafii Badr Aldiyn Aleaynii (Died: 855 H) , **Publisher:** Dar Alkutub Alilmia Beirut, Lebanon, 1st Edition , 1420 H-2000 CE.

Taj AlUrus Min Jawahir AlQamus , Muhammad Bin Mhmad Bin Abd Alrazaaqaq Alhusaynii , 'Abu Alfayd , nicknamed as Murtadaa , AlZabydy (Died: 1205 H) , **Editor:** Group of Editors , **Publisher:** Dar AlHidayah.

Tarikh Baghdad, 'Abu Bakr 'Ahmad Bin Ealiin Thabit Bin 'Ahmad Bin Mahdii Alkhatib Albaghdadii (Died: 463 H), **Editor:** Dr. Bashaar Awad Maruf , **Publisher:** Dar Algharb Al'iislami-Beirut , 1st Edition , 1422 H / 2002 CE.

Tarikh Dimishq , 'Abu Alqasim Ali Bin Alhasan well known as Ibn Asakir (Died: 571 H) , **Editor:** Amru Bin Gharamat AlUumrawii , **Publisher:** Dar Alfikr For Printing, Publishing & Distribution **Year of Publishing:** 1415 H-1995 CE.

Altibyan Fi Adaab Hamlat AlQuran , 'Abu Zakariaa Muhyi Aldiyn Yahyaa Bin Sharaf AlNawawii (Died: 676 H) , **Edited & Annotated by:** Muhamad Alhajaar , 3rd Edition, 1414 H-1994 CE , **Publisher:** Dar Hazm For Printing, Publishing and Distribution, Beirut, Lebanon.

Tabyin Alhaqayiq Sharh Kanz Aldaqayiq Wahashiat Alshalabii , Uthman Bin Alii Bin Mahjin Albarieii , Fakhr Aldiyn Alzayleii Alhanafii (Died: 743 H) , **Footnotes:** Shihab Aldiyn 'Ahmad Bin Muhamad Bin 'Ahmad Bin Yunis Bin 'Iismaeil Bin Yunis Alshalabi (Died: 1021 H) , **Publisher:** AlMatbaeat Alkubraa Al'amiriat- Bawlaq , Cairo , 1st Edition , 1313 H.

Tafsir Aibn 'Abi Hatim - Tafsir AlQuran Alazim , 'Abu Muhamad Abd Alrahman Bin Muhamad Bin 'Iidris Bin Almundhir Altamimi , Alhanzalii , Alraazi Aibn 'Abi Hatim (Died: 327 H) , **Editor:** 'Asad Muhamad Altayib , **Publisher:** Maktabat Nizar Mustafaa Albaz, KSA , 3rd Edition 1419 H.

Tafsir ibn Juzay - Altashil Lieulum Altanzil, 'Abu Alqasim , Muhamad Bin 'Ahmad Bin Muhamad Bin Abd Allah , Ibn Juzay Alkalbi Algharnatii (Died: 741 H) , **Editor:** Dr. Abdallah Alkhalidi , **Publisher:** Dar Al'arqam Bin 'Abi Al'arqam-Beirut , 1st Edition , 1416 H

Tafsir ibn Ashur - Altahrir Waltanwir , Muhamad Altaahir Bin Muhamad Bin Muhamad Altaahir Bin Ashur AlTunusii (Died: 1393 H) , **Publisher:** AlDaar AlTuwnisiat Lilnashr -Tunis , **Year of Publishing:** 1984 H.

Tafsir Ibn Atiyyah - Almuharir Alwajiz Fi Tafsir Alkitaab Alaziz , 'Abu Muhamad Abdalhaq Bin Ghalib Bin Abdalrahman Bin Tamaam Bin Atiat Al'andalusi Almuharibii (Died: 542 H) , **Editor:** Abdalsalam Abdalshaafi Muhamad , **Publisher:** Dar Alkutub Al-Ilmiyah , Beirut , 1st Edition , 1422 H.

Tafsir Ibn Kathir - Tafsir AlQuran AlAzim, 'Abu Alfida' 'Iismaeil Bin Umar Bn Kathir Alqurashi Albasri Thuma Aldimashqi (Died: 774 H) , **Editor:** Sami Bin Muhamad Salamah , **Publisher:** Dar Taybah for Publishing and Distribution , 2nd Edition 1420 H- 1999 CE.

Tafsir 'Abi Hayaan - Albahr Almuhit Fit Tafsir: 'Abu Hayaan Muhamad Bin Yusif Bin Hayaan 'Uthir Aldeen Al'Andalusi (Died: 745 H) , **Editor:** Sidqi Muhamad Jamil , **Publisher:** Dar Alfikr -Beirut , **Year of Publication:** 1420 H.

Tafsir Albaghawii - Ma'alim Altanzil Fi Tafsir AlQuran , Reviver of the Sunnah , 'Abu Muhamad Alhusayn Bin Masud Bin Muhamad

Bin Muhamad Bin Muhamad Bin 'Abi Harir Albaghawii Alshaafi (Died: 510 H) , **Editor:** Abdalrazaaq Almahdi , **Publisher:** Dar 'Iihya' Alturath AlArabi -Beirut , 1st Edition , 1420 H.

Tafsir Albaydawii - 'Anwar Altanzil Wa'asrar Altaawil , Nasir Addeen 'Abu Saeid Abdallah Bin Umar Bin Muhamad Alshiyrazi Albaydawi (Died: 685 H) , **Editor:** Muhamad Abdalrahman Almar'ashali , **Publisher:** Dar 'Iihya' Alturath AlArabi -Beirut , 1st Edition / 1418 H.

Tafsir Altha'labii - Alkashf Walbayan 'An Tafsir AlQuran , 'Ahmad Bin 'Iibrahim Althaelabii (Died: 427 H) , **Takhreej Supervision:** Dr. Salah Baa-uthman , Dr. Hasan Alghazali , Dr. Zayd Muharish , Dr. Amin Bashah , **Editor:** Group of Researchers , **Publisher:** Dar Altafsir , Jeddah, KSA, 1st Edition , 1436 H-2015 CE.

Tafsir Alraazi - Altafsir Alkabir - Mafatih Alghayb , 'Abu Abdallah Muhamad Bin Umar Bin Alhusayn Bin Alhusayn Altaymi Alraazi nicknamed as Fakhr Aldeen AlRaazii Khatib Alrayi (Died: 606 H) , **Publisher:** Dar 'Iihya' Alturath AlArabi -Beirut , 3rd Edition , 1420 H.

Tafsir Alraaghib Al'asfahani , 'Abu Alqasim Alhusayn Bin Muhamad Almaeruf Bialraaghib Al'asfahanii , Aljuz' 1: Almuqadimat Watafsir Alfatihat Walbaqarat , **Edited & Reviewed:** Dr. Muhamad Abdialeaziz Basyuni , **Publisher:** Kuliyat Aladab-Jamieat Tanta , 1st Edition: 1420 H-1999 CE , Juz' 2 , 3: Min 'Awal Surat Al Eimran -Whataa Alayat 113 Min Surat Alnisa' , **Edited & Reviewed:** Du. Eadil Bin Eali Alshidi , **Publisher:** Dar Alwatan - Alriyad , 1st Edition: 1424 H-2003m , Juz' 4 , 5: (Min Alayat 114 Min Surat Alnisa' -Whataa Akhir Surat Almayida) , **Edited & Reviewed:** Dr. Hind Bint Muhamad Bin Zahid Sardar , **Publisher:** Kuliyat Aldaewat Wa'usul Aldiyn -Jamieat 'Amm Alquraa , 1st Edition: 1422 Hi-2001m.

Tafsir Alzamakhshari - Alkashaf An Haqayiq Ghawamid Altanzil , 'Abu Alqasim Mahmud Bin 'Ahmad , Alzamakhashari Jaar Allah (Died: 538 H) , **Publisher:** Dar Alkitaab AlArabi -Beirut , 3rd Edition , 1407 H.

Tafsir Alshanqitii - 'Adwa' Albayan Fi 'Iidah AlQuran BiAlQuran , Muhamad Al'amin Bin Muhamad Almukhtar Bin Abdalqadir Aljakni Alshanqitii (Died: 1393 H) , **Publisher:** Dar Alfikr For Printing, Publishing & Distribution , Beirut -Lebanon , **Year of Publishing:** 1415 H-1995 CE.

Tafsir AlTabari - Jami Albayan Ean Tawil Ayat AlQuran , **Editor:** Dr. Abdallah Bin Abdalmuhsin AtTurki , Project with Markaz Albuhuth Waldirasat Al'iislamiat Bidar Hajr Alduktur Abdalsand Hasan Yamamah , **Publisher:** Dar Hajr For Printing, Publishing, Distribution and Advertisement , 1st Edition , 1422 H-2001 CE.

Tafsir AlQurtubii – AlJami' LiAhkam AlQuran , 'Abu Abdallah Muhamad Bin 'Ahmad Bin 'Abi Bakr Bin Farah AlAnsari Alkhazraji Shams Aldeen AlQurtubii (Died: 671 H) , **Editor:** Ahmad AlBarduni Waibrahim 'Atfish , **Publisher:** Dar Alkutub AlMasriyah - Cairo , 2nd Edition , 1384 H- 1964 CE.

Tafsir Almawardi - Alnukt WalUyun , 'Abu Alhasan Eali Bin Muhamad Bin Muhamad Bin Habib Albasarii Albaghdadii , also known as Almawardii (Died: 450 H) , **Editor:** Alsayid Bin Abd Almaqsud Bin Abd Alrahim , **Publisher:** Dar Alkutub Al-Ilmiyah - Beirut / Lebanon.

Tafsir AlQuran , 'Abu Bakr Muhamad Bin 'Iibrahim Bin Almundhir Alnaysaburii (Died: 319 H) , Edited and Reviewed by Dr. Sad Bin Muhamad AlSad , **Publisher:** Dar Almathir -Madinah Munawwarah , 1st Edition, 1423 H - 2002 CE.

Tanbih Alghafilin An 'Amal Aljahilin Watahdhir Alsaalikin Min 'Afal Aljahilin , Muhyi Aldeen 'Abu Zakariaa 'Ahmad Bin 'Iibrahim Bin Alnahaas Aldimashqii (Died: 814 H) , **Edited & Annotated:** Imad Aldeen Abbas Saeid , 'Iishrafa: Alsalaf Almaktabii Lilturath , **Publisher:** Dar Alkutub Al-Ilmiyah , Beirut -Lebanon , 1st Edition , 1407 H.

Tahdhib Allughah , Muhamad Bin 'Ahmad Bin Al'azharii Alharawii , 'Abu Mansur (Died: 370 H) , **Editor:** Muhamad Eawad Mureib , **Publisher:** Dar 'Iihya' Alturath AlArabi -Beirut , 1st Edition , 2001 CE.

Jamie Alrasayil , Taqi Aldiyn 'Abu AlAbbaas 'Ahmad Bin Abd Alhalim Bin Abdalsalam Bin Taymia Alharaanii Alhanbali Aldimashqii (Died: 728 H) , **Editor:** Du. Muhamad Rashad Salim , **Publisher:** Dar Alaata' -Alriyadh , 1st Edition 1422 H-2001m.

Jamie Bayan Al'ilm Wafaddluh , 'Abu umar Yusif Bin Abdallah Bin Muhamad Bin abdalbir Bin Asim Alnamrii AlQurtibii (Died: 463 H) , **Editor:** 'Abi Al'ashbal Alzuhiri , **Publisher:** Dar Aibn Aljawzi , KSA , 1st Edition , 1414 H-1994 CE.

Aljawab Alsahih Liman Badal Din Almasih , Taqi Aldiyn 'Abu Alabbas 'Ahmad Bin Abd Alhalim Bin Abdalsalam Bin Abdallah Bin 'Abi Alqasim Bin Muhamad Bin Taymia Alharaanii Alhanbali Aldimashqii (Died: 728 H) , **Editor:** Ali Bin Hasan -Abd Alaziz Bin 'Iibrahim -Hamdan Bin Muhammad , **Publisher:** Dar Aleasimah , KSA , 2nd Edition , 1419 H-1999 CE.

Hilyat Al'awlia' Watabaqat Al'asfia' , 'Abu Naeim 'Ahmad Bin Abdallah Bin 'Ahmad Bin 'Ishaq Bin Musaa Bin Mihran Al'asbhanii (Died: 430 H) , **Publisher:** Alsaeadah - Bjiwar Muhafazat Egypt , 1394 Hi / 1974 CE.

Aldurr Almanthur , Abdalrahman Bin 'Abi Bakr , Jalal Aldiyn Alsuyutii (Died: 911 H) , **Publisher:** Dar Alfikr -Birut.

Aldurar Alsaniyya Fi Al'ajwibat Alnajdiah , ulama' Najid Al'aelam , **Editor:** Abdalrahman Bin Muhamad Bin Qasim , 6th Edition , 1417 H-1996m.

Diwan 'Abi 'Iishaq Al'iilbiriu , 'Iibrahim Bin Maseud Bin Saeid , 'Abu 'Iishaq Altajibiu Al'iilbiry (Died: 460 H) , **Editor:** Dr. Muhamad Ridwan Aldaaya , **Publisher:** Dar Qutaiba - Damascus , 2nd Edition , 1401 H-1981m.

Alrihlat Fi Talab Alhadith , 'Abu Bakr 'Ahmad Bin ali bin Thabit Bin 'Ahmad Bin Mahdii Alkhatib Albaghdadii (Died: 463 H) , **Editor:** Nur Aldiyn Atr , **Publisher:** Dar Alkutub Al-Ilmiyah – Beirut, 1st Edition, 1395 H.

Rawayie Altafsir (Aljamie Litafsir Al'iimam ibn Rajab Alhanbali) , Zayn Aldiyn Bin 'Ahmad Bin Rajab Bn Alhasan , Alsalamy , Albaghdadi , Thuma Aldimashqii , Alhanbali (Died: 795 H) , **Compiled:** 'Abi Muadh Tariq Bin awad Allah Bin Muhamad , **Publisher:** Dar Alasimah -KSA, 1st Edition, 1422 H-2001m.

Zad Almaaad Fi Hady Khayr Alabaad , Muhamad Bin 'Abi Bakr Bin Saed Shams Aldiyn Aibn Qiam Aljawzia (Died: 751 H) , **Publisher:** Muasasat Alrisalah , Beirut -Maktabat Almanar Al'iislamiah , Kuweit , 27th Edition , 1415 H-1994 CE.

Silsilat Al'ahadith Alsahihat Washay' Min Fiqhiha Wafawayidiha , **Author:** Muhamad Nasir Aldeen Bin Alhaj Nuh Bin Najaati Bin Adim , Al'ashqudaniu (Died: 1420 H) , **Publisher:** Maktabat Almaearif Lilnashr Waltawzie , Riyadh , 1st Edition.

Sunan ibn Majah , 'Abu Abdallah Muhamad Bin Yazid Alqazwini (Died: 273 H) , **Editor:** Muhamad Fuad Abdalbaqi , **Publisher:** Dar 'Iihya' Alkutub Alearabiat -Faysal Eisaa Albabi Alhalabi.

Sunan Abi Dawud , 'Abi Dawud Sulayman Bin Al'asheath Bin 'Iishaq Bin Bashir (Died: 275 H) , **Editor:** Muhamad Muhyi Aldiyn Abdalhamid , **Publisher:** Almaktabat Alasriah , Sayda -Birut.

Sunan Altirmidhii , Muhamad Bn Eisaa Bn Surat Bin Musaa Bn Aldahaak , Altirmidhiu , 'Abu Eisaa (Died: 279 Hi) , **Editor:** Du. Bashaar Eawad Maeruf , **Publisher:** Dar Algharb Al'iislami-Birut , **Year of Publication:** 1998 CE.

Siyar 'Aelam Alnubala' , Shams Aldiyn 'Abu Abdallah Muhamad Bin 'Ahmad Bin Euthman Bin Qaymaz Aldhahabii (Died: 748 H) , **Editor:** Group of Researchers unders supervision of Alshaykh Shuayb Al'arnawuwt , **Publisher:** Muasasat Alrisalah , 3rd Edition , 1405 H-1985 CE.

Sharah Altaybi Ealaa Mishkat Alkamiyaat Almusamaa Bi (Alkashif Ean Haqayiq Alsunan) , Sharaf Aldeen Alhusayn Bin Abd Allah Altaybi (D: 743 H) , **Editor:** Dr. Abdalhamid Hindawi , **Publisher:** Maktabat Nizar Mustafaa Albaz (Makkah, Riyadh) , 1st Edition , 1417 H-1997 CE.

Sharh Riad Alsaalihin , Muhamad Bin Salih Bin Muhamad Aluthaymin (Died: 1421 H) , **Publisher:** Dar Alwatan Lilnashr , Riyadh , Edition: 1426 H.

Sharh Sahih Albukharii LiIbn Bataal , Abn Bataal 'Abu Alhasan Ealii Bn Khalaf Bn Abdalmalik (Died: 449 H) , **Editor:** 'Abu Tamim Yasir Bn 'Iibrahim , **Publisher:** Maktabat Alrushd – Riyadh, KSA , 2nd Edition , 1423 H- 2003 CE.

Shu'b Al'iiman , 'Ahmad Bin Alhusayn Bin Ealii Bin Musaa Alkhusrujardi Alkhurasanii , 'Abu Bakr Albayhaqi (Died: 458 H) , **Reviewed & Researched by:** Dr. Abd Alali Abd Alhamid Hamid , **Publisher:** Maktabat Alrushd Lilnashr Waltawzie, Riyadh, Project with Aldaar Alsalafiat Bibumba, India, 1st Edition , 1423 H-2003m.

Alsihah Taj Allughat Wasihah AlAarabia , 'Abu Nasr 'Iismaeil Bin Hamaad Aljawharii Alfarabi (Died: 393 H) , **Editor:** 'Ahmad Abd Alghafur Eataar , **Publisher:** Dar Alilm Lilmalayin -Beirut , 4rth Edition: 1407 H-1987m.

Sahih Al'adab Almufrad Lil'iimam Albukharii , Muhamad Bin 'Iismaeil Bin 'Iibrahim Bin Almughirat Albukharii , 'Abu Abdallah (Died: 256 H) , **Ahadith researched and annotated by:** Muhamad Nasir Aldiynani , **Publisher:** Dar Alsiddiq Lilnashr Waltawzie , 4rth Edition , 1418 H -1997 CE.

Sahih Albukharii - Aljamie Almusnad Alsahih Almukhtasar Min 'Umur Rasul Allah Wasunanih Wa'ayaamuh , Muhamad Bin 'Iismaeil 'Abu Abdallah Albukhari Aljuefi , **Editor:** Muhamad Zuhayr Bin Nasir Alnaasir , **Publisher:** Dar Tawq Alnajaa , **Numbering:** Muhamad Fuad Abd Albaqi , 1st Edition , 1422 H.

Sahih Altarghib Waltarhib , Muhamad Nasir Aldiyn Al'albani (Died: 1420 H) , **Publisher:** Maktabat Almaearif - Riyadh , 5th Edition

Sahih Muslim - Almusnid Almukhtasar Alsahih Binaql Aladl 'Iilaa Rasul Allah , Muslim Bn Alhajaaj 'Abu Alhasan Alqushayrii Alnaysaburii (Died: 261 H) , **Editor:** Muhamad Fuad Abdalbaqi , **Publisher:** Dar 'Iihya' Alturath AlArabi , Beirut.

Sayd Alkhatir , Jamal Aldiyn 'Abu Alfaraj Abd Alrahman Bin Alii Bin Muhamad Aljawzii (Died: 597 H) , **Supervised:** Hasan Almasahi Suaydan , **Publisher:** Dar Alqalam - Damascus , 1st Edition , 1425 H-2004m.

Daeif Sunan Altirmidhii , Muhamad Nasir Aldiyn Al'albanii (Died: 1420 Hi) , **Printing & Annotation Supervised by:** Zuhayr Alshaawish , **Distribution:** Almaktab Al'iislamii -Beirut , 1st Edition , 1411 H-1991 CE.

Tabaqat Alshaafieia Alkubraa , Abd Alwahaab Bn Taqi Aldiyn Alsabakia (Died: 771 H) , **Editor:** Dr. Mahmud Muhamad Altanahi Dr. Abd Alfataah Muhamad Alhulw , **Publisher:** Hajar For Printing, Publishing & Distribution , 2nd Edition , 1413 H.

Tarah Altathrib Fi Sharh Altaqrib , 'Abu Alfadl Abdalrahim Bin Alhusayn Bin Abdalrahman Bin 'Iibrahim Aleiraqii (Died: 806 H) , 'Akmalah Aibnuhu: 'Ahmad Bin Abdalrahim Bin Alhusayn Alkurdi Alraaziani Thuma Almisriu , 'Abu Zarat Wali Aldiyn , ibn Aliraqii (Died: 826 H) , **Publisher:** AlMasriyah AlQadimah.

Tariq Alhijratayn Wabab Alsaeadatayn , Muhamad Bin 'Abi Bakr Bin Saed Abn Qiam Aljawzia (Died: 751 H) , **Publisher:** Dar Alsalafiat , Cairo , Egypt , 2nd Edition , 1394 H.

Aadat AlQuran Al'uslubia Dirasat Tatbiqiah, Rashid Bin Hamuwd Bin Rashid Althanyan , **Publisher:** Dar Altadamuriah , Aljamia Alsaudia Lilquran Waulumih, 1st Edition , 1432 H.

Aridat Al'ahwadhi Bisharh Sahih Altirmidhii , 'Abu Bakr AlArabi Almalikiu , **Editor:** Jamal Maraeashaliun , **Publisher:** Dar Alkutub Al-Ilmiyah , **Year of Publicationi:** 1418 H-1997 CE , 1st Edition.

Aladhb Alnamayr Min Majalis Alshanqitii Fi Altafsir , Muhamad Al'amin Bin Muhamad Almukhtar Bin Abd Alqadir Aljaknii Alshanqitii (Died: 1393 H) ,**Supervised by:** Dr. Bakr Bin Abdallah 'Abu Zayd , **Publisher:** Dar Ealam Alfawayid Lilnashr Waltawzie , Makah Almukaramah , 2nd Edition , 1426 H.

Al'Uqubat , 'Abu Bakr Abd Allh Bin Muhamad Bin Eubayd Bin Sifyan Bin Qays Albaghdadii Al'umawii Alqurashiu well known as Ibn 'Abi Aldunya (Died: 281 H) , Died 281 H , **Editor:** Muhamad Khayr Ramadan Yusuf , **Publisher:** Dar ibn Hazam , Beirut -Lebanon , 1st Edition , 1416 H-1996 CE.

Alayn , Almansub Li'abi Abdalrahman Alkhalil Bin 'Ahmad Bin Eamriw Bin Tamim Alfarahidii Albasari (Died: 170 H) , **Editor:** Dr. Mahdi Almakhzumi , Dr. 'Iibrahim Alsaamaraayiy , **Publisher:** Dar Wamaktabat Alhilal.

Fatah Albari Sharh Sahih Albukharii , 'Ahmad Bin ali Bin Hajar 'Abu Alfadl AlAasqalani Alshaafi , **Publisher:** Dar Almaerifa -Beirut , 1379 , **Numbering of Chapters and Ahadith:** Muhamad Fuad Abdalbaqi , **Editing and Supervision:** Muhibu Aldiyn Khateeb , **Annotation:** Abdalaziz Bin Abdallah Bin Bazi.

Fath Almughith Bisharh 'Alfiat Alhadith Lileiraqii , Shams Aldiyn 'Abu Alkhayr Muhamad Bin Abdalrahman Bin Muhamad Alsakhawi (Died: 902 H), **Editor:** Ali Husayn Ali , **Publisher:** Maktabat Alsanat - Egypt , 1st Edition , 1424 Hi / 2003 CE.

Fadayil Alsahabat , 'Abu Abdallah 'Ahmad Bin Muhamad Bin Hanbal Bin Hilal Bin 'Asad Alshaybani (Died: 241 H) , **Editor:** Da. Wasi Allah Muhamad Eabaas , **Publisher:** Muasasat Alrisalah - Beirut , 1st Edition , 1403 H-1983 CE.

Fayd Alqadir Sharh Aljamie Alsaghir , Zayan Aldiyn Muhamad known as Abd Alrawuwf Bin Taj AlArifin Bin Ali Bin Aali AlAabidin Alhadaadii Thuma Almanawi Alqahiri (Died: 1031 H) , **Publisher:** Almaktabat Altijariat Alkubraa -Egypt , 1st Edition, 1356 ٠.

Qiladat Alnahr Fi Wafayat 'Aeyan Aldahr , 'Abu Muhamad Altayib Bin Abdalllh Bin 'Ahmad Bin Ealii Biamkharimat , Alhijrany Alhadramii Alshaafieii (870-947 h) , **Supervised:** Bu Jumeat Makri / Khalid Zawari , **Publisher:** Dar Alminhaj -Jdat , 1st Edition , 1428 H-2008 CE

Qawaid Qawaid Fi Masalih Al'anam , 'Abu Muhamad Eizi Aldiyn , Maktabat Alkuliyaat Al'azhariat , (Wasuaratuha Dawr Eidat Mithla:

Dar Alkutub) Al-Ilmiyah -Beirut , Wadar 'Am Alquraa -Cairo, **Edition:** Revised Updated Edition, 1414 H-1991 CE.

Latayif Almaearif Limawasim Aleam Min Alwazayif , Zayn Aldiyn Abd Alrahman Bin 'Ahmad Bin Rajab Bin Alhasan , Alsalamii , Albaghdadii , Thuma Aldimashqii , Alhanbali (Died: 795 H) , **Publisher:** Dar ibn Hazam For Printing And Publishing: 1st Edition , 1424 H-2004 CE.

Almujtabaa Min Alsunan - Alsunan Alsughraa Lilnisayiyi , 'Abu Abd 'Ahmad Bin Shueayb Bin Alrahman Alkhurasanii , Alnasayi (Died: 303 H) , **Editor:** Abd Alfataah 'Abu Ghudda , **Publisher:** Maktab Almatbuat -Halab , 2nd Edition , 1406 H-1986 CE.

Mujmal Allughat , 'Ahmad Bin Faris Bin Zakaria' Alqazwinii Alraazii , 'Abu Alhusayn (Died: 395 H) , **Edited:** Zuhayr Abd Almuhsin Sultan , **Publisher:** Muasasat Alrisalah -Beirut , 2nd Edition -1406 H-1986 CE.

Majmu Fatawaa Shaykh Al'islam 'Ahmad Aibn Taymiah , Compiled **by:** Abdalrahman Bin Muhamad Bin Qasim , Majma' Almalik Fahd Litibaeat Almushaf Alsharif , Madinah Almunawarah , 1416 H.

Madarij Alsaalikin Bayn Manazil 'Iiaak Naebud Wa'iiaak Nastaein , Muhamad Almutasim Billah Albaghdadi , **Publisher:** Dar Alkitaab AlArabi -Beirut , 3rd Edition , 1416 H-1996 CE.

Musnad Al'iimam 'Ahmad Bin Hanbal , 'Abu Abdallah 'Ahmad Bin Muhamad Bin Hanbal Bin Hilal Bin 'Asad Alshaybani (Died: 241 H) , **Editor:** Shuayb Al'Arnawuwt - adil Murshid , Wakhrun , 'Iishrafi: ' Dr. Abdallah Bin Abdalmuhsin Alturki , **Publisher:** Muasasat Alrisalah , 1st Edition , 1421 H / 2001 CE

Musanaf Abd Alrazaaq Alsaneanii , 'Abu Bakr Abd Alrazaaq Bin Humam Bin Nafie Alhimyari Alyamanii Alsananii (126-211hi) ,

Tahqiq Habib Alrahman Al'azamii , Issued from Almaktab Al'iislamii BiBeirut , Sanat, 1403 H.

Almutalae Alaa 'Alfaz Almuqanae , Muhamad Bn 'Abi Alfatha: Maktabat Alsawadi Liltawzie , 1st Edition, 1423 Hi-2003m.

Mujam Al'udaba' - 'Iirshad Al'arshad 'Iilaa Maerifat Al'adib , Shihab Aldeen 'Abu Abdallah Yaqut Bin Abdallah Alrumi Alhamawi (Died: 626 H) , **Editor:** 'Iihsan abbaas , **Publisher:** Dar Algharb Al'iislamii , Beirut , 1st Edition , 1414 H-1993 CE.

Maqasid Alsharieat Al'iislamiat , Muhamad Altaahir Bin Muhamad Bin Muhamad Altaahir Bin Eashur Altuwnusii (Died: 1393 H) , **Editor:** Muhamad Alhabib Bin Alkhawjat , Ministry of Islamic affair and endowments, **Year of Publishing:** 1425 H-2004 CE.

Maqayis Allughah , 'Ahmad Bin Faris Bin Zakaria' Alqazwinii Alraazii , 'Abu Alhusayn (Died: 395 H) , **Edited by:** Abd Alsalam Muhamad Harun , **Publisher:** Dar Alfikr , **Year of Publishing:** 1399 H-1979 CE.

Alminhaj Sharh Sahih Muslim Bin Alhajaaj - Sharh Alnawawii alaa Muslim , 'Abu Zakariaa Muhyi Aldeen Yahyaa Bin Sharaf Alnawawi (Died: 676 H) , **Publisher:** Dar 'Iihya' Alturath AlArabi -Beirut , 2nd Edition , 1392 H.

Almuwafaqat , 'Iibrahim Bin Musaa Bin Muhammad Allakhmi Algharnati well known as Bilshaatibii (Died: 790 H) , **Editor:** 'Abu Eubaydat Mashhur Bin Hasan Al Salman , **Publisher:** Dar ibn affaan , 1st Edition 1417 H-1997 CE.

Nuzm Aldarar Fi Tanasub Alayat Walsuwar , 'Iibrahim Bn Eumar Bn Hasan Alribat Bn Eali 'Abi Bakr Albiqaeii (Died: 885 H) , **Publisher:** Dar Alkitaab Al'iislamii , Cairo.

Alnakt Fi 'Iiejaz AlQuran , Ali Bin Eisaa Bin Abd Allah , 'Abu Alhasan Alrumaanii Almuetazilii (Died: 384 H) , **Editor:** Muhamad Khalaf Allah , Dr. Muhamad Zaghlul Salam , **Publisher:** Dar Almaarif in Cairo , 3rd Edition , 1976 CE.